CANADIAN TELEVISION TODAY

CANADIAN TELEVISION TODAY

Bart Beaty and Rebecca Sullivan

Op/Position: Issues and Ideas series, No. 1

UNIVERSITY OF
CALGARY
PRESS

© 2006 Bart Beaty and Rebecca Sullivan

Published by the University of Calgary Press

2500 University Drive NW

Calgary, Alberta, Canada T2N 1N4

www.uofcpress.com

Library and Archives Canada Cataloguing in Publication

Beaty, Bart

Canadian television today / Bart Beaty and Rebecca Sullivan.

(Op/Position : issues and ideas ; 1)

Includes bibliographical references and index.

ISBN 1-55238-222-2 (pbk.)

1. Television—Social aspects—Canada. 2. Television—Canada. I. Sullivan, Rebecca, 1966- II. Title. III. Series.

PN1992.3.C3B33 2006   302.23'450971   C2006-903923-2

We acknowledge the financial support of the Government of Canada, through the Book Publishing Industry Development Program (BPIDP), and the Alberta Foundation for the Arts for our publishing activities. We acknowledge the support of the Canada Council for the Arts for our publishing program.

Canadä

Printed and bound in Canada by AGMV Marquis

∞This book is printed on 60 lb. Rolland Enviro 100 natural text

Cover design, page design and typesetting by Mieka West

TABLE OF CONTENTS

PREFACE

This book is our effort to raise important questions about Canadian media, culture and society and to reach beyond traditional academic borders. The research here derives from work that we have done for the first two volumes of *How Canadians Communicate*, an anthology of essays specifically addressing the contemporary status of Canada's cultural industries and institutions. In contributing to those volumes we found that we have been somewhat constrained by the brevity of our articles, always desiring to explore the implications of our arguments more fully. This is what we have sought to accomplish with *Canadian Television Today*. Rather than writing another history of Canadian television policy, or a journal-length examination of a few chosen contemporary television programs, we have written a work that is neither fully one nor the other. Too long to be a series of journal articles, too brief to be a typical academic monograph, we invite the reader to regard this work as an extended essay that asks the question "Where is Canadian television today? And what are the implications of its current status as Canadians move into the future?" In that spirit, then, we address this book to scholars engaged in issues of media, technology, cultural policy, identity, and nationhood. But we also hope that this book will reach beyond the academic milieu and offer all Canadians the opportunity to discuss more fully the extent of their engagement with the way society is culturally and technologically mediated by television and how one can do better in opening up Canada to multiple voices through this medium.

ACKNOWLEDGEME

S

Our initial collaborative writing on Canadian television took the form of contributions to the first two volumes of How Canadians Communicate. These books were thoughtfully orchestrated by Maria Bakardjieva, Frits Pannekoek, and David Taras. We are grateful to them for asking us to think more deeply about the present state of Canadian television, and for placing us on the road that culminated in this work. We would also like to thank Joseph Jackson, now a too-distant colleague and friend, for extending to us an invitation to address the Lincoln Commission in 2002. This was a formative experience in the development of our argument in these pages.

This book would not have happened were it not for a conversation between the authors and Walter Hildebrandt, former director of the University of Calgary Press. Walter's vision of a new series of timely books addressing salient issues in Canadian society became the basis for the Op/Position series, and we would not have undertaken this work without his enthusiasm for the topic. We have great respect for Walter's commitment to scholarly excellence, and extend our deepest thanks to him for his work on this project.

Bart Beaty would like to particularly thank the Killam Foundation, whose provision of a Killam Resident Fellowship in 2004 provided the requisite time to work on an earlier draft of this manuscript.

We would also like to thank Ann Smith and Marie Babey for their work on the final manuscript.

Our families have been a tremendous source of support over the course of our professional and private lives together. We especially want to thank our son, Sebastian, who arrived in our lives while this book was being prepared and whose presence allows us to keep these issues in perspective.

Finally, we would like to dedicate this work to our teachers at McGill University, Gertrude Robinson and Will Straw. They represent the best of Canadian scholarship, and shared with us their deep commitment to the pursuit of knowledge. Their work on mass media systems, and particularly on the important role that Canadian media have played in the construction of the nation, serves as the foundation upon which we have sought to build. We hope this book honours them for their uncompromising vision of academic research in service to the public good.

INTRODUCTION: CANA

N TELEVISION TODAY

Some may well ask, in this age of conglomeration and media convergence, why bother with a book solely on television? This book is itself an answer to that very question, centrally addressing itself to the issue of how television functions in Canada and matters to Canadians, at this moment in time. That said, there is no short answer to the question: Why? The answer revolves around a series of concerns that range from technology to politics, and from economic futures to cultural traditions. Since the first signals hit the air, broadcasting has played a key role – some would argue the primary role – in defining how Canadians understand themselves as a people. Successive governmental commissions have debated the role of broadcasting in the formation and maintenance of Canada as a sovereign nation-state since the Aird Commission in 1932, which established the conditions for the creation of the Canadian Radio Broadcasting Corporation (later, the Canadian Broadcasting Corporation or CBC), and each has arrived at the conclusion that Canada requires a healthy broadcast infrastructure in order to maintain national cohesiveness. As a result of this governmental prodding, Canada has developed one of the most impressive telecommunication networks in the world, but one which nonetheless has often been criticized for failing in its major duty of bringing Canadian stories to Canadian people. The real culprit, say cultural nationalists, is American broadcasting, which casts a long shadow over "our" territory and lures away audiences with its flashier product. Others respond that the problem is internal, that second-rate local programming is so dull it can't compete with American network fare. Now, new wireless, digital, and streaming technologies threaten the very existence of television as a distinct medium that can be controlled through regulatory frameworks and governmental policy. Some see this as a problem that requires even greater governmental oversight. We take a decidedly different position. We refuse to perceive Canadian television as the righteous underdog to American domination. Further, we refuse to conceive of television as a provider of discrete, identifiable national culture that is served up to a passive audience. At this current moment in history, television is a revealing object of inquiry because the threat of its own obsolescence – whether political, technological, or economic – serves to highlight a number of intriguing possibilities for rethinking concepts like national culture, media hegemony, and the mass audience.

THE FIELD OF CANADIAN TELEVISION STUDIES

In 2001, when we first began looking into the state of Canadian television, what struck us most was the lack of attention it has received from scholars and critics. Even as the Canadian Radio-television and Telecommunications Commission (CRTC) was setting up the largest expansion of channel offerings in the world, and court cases were being filed by cable and satellite companies to control how Canadians would receive those channels, the significance of these changes warranted little attention outside the halls of policy makers. The debates, such as they were, played out in submissions to regulators and on the dials of our television sets. The issues had been dealt with more forcefully in the practice of television viewers than in the theories of television scholars. In fact, much of the contemporary literature available on Canadian television comes from governmental agencies. The most important recent study is *Our Cultural Sovereignty*, the culmination of two years of hearings on the future of Canadian broadcasting by the House of Commons Standing Committee on Heritage. Since its release in 2003, the report has mostly languished in the back offices of parliamentary interns, with only occasional signs of life, and little attention has been paid to its many recommendations. Relying upon political committees to draft the parameters for the public debate on culture (a tendency that has a long history in this country) highlights a major absence in critical cultural debates. In November 2002, we testified before the Lincoln committee that drafted *Our Cultural Sovereignty*. It did not go well. The members of Parliament were easily distracted by their pet issues and the issues of their campaign contributors, and we had little sense that anything of substance had been communicated by us to the committee members in the question and answer panel format of the hearings. This book, then, is our effort to put on paper what we wanted to tell the committee that morning in Ottawa.

We intend this book to be an intervention into the small body of scholarly literature dedicated to exploring Canadian television, and into the wider literature that examines the implications of the medium for Canadian culture more generally. Sadly, much of this writing fails to avoid the trap of nationalist navel gazing and extend the debate about television onto the global stage. To our minds, this is an unfortunate oversight given Canadian television's unique positioning in the economic, political, and cultural life of this country. More importantly, the history, present condition, and future promise of Canadian television offer a completely different way of thinking about cultural issues in international and local, as well as national contexts.

Most of the books on Canadian television that do exist were published before the recent technological revolution brought on by the internet and new digital technologies. Perhaps the best of these is by a British scholar. Richard Collins' *Culture, Communication and National Identity: The Case of Canadian Television* (1990) is now more than fifteen years old, but although some of his examples have become outdated, the ideas behind them are not. Collins uses the lens of television to explore the decoupling of polity from culture, the encroachment of globalizing forces on national borders, and the invocation of the audience as both/either consumer and citizen. In many ways, we are seeking to continue the conversation he started that was somewhat rudely inter-rupted by an exploding telecommunications network. However, un-like Collins, we are not going to rehash the histories of the CBC and the CRTC – stories that have been told many times already and which, to our mind, prevent the conversation from moving forward. Also, while Collins hints at the coming forces of globalization and technological convergence, the implications of these shifts were in no way as widely felt then as they are now.

Two of the more current and lively contributions to television studies in Canada are David Hogarth's *Documentary Television in Canada: From National Public Service to Global Marketplace* (2002), and *On Location: Canada's Television Industry in a Global Marketplace* by Serra Tinic (2005). Both books emphasize the importance of under-standing Canadian television on aesthetic and economic grounds in relation to vast changes in international market trends. The expansion of television as an increasingly global, rather than national, medium has opened up new possibilities in co-productions and increased audi-ence potential. At the same time, it also creates problems for produc-ers looking to create culturally specific dramatic or documentary pro-gramming. It also, importantly, puts to the test national funding, spon-sorship, and subsidy programs in defining what counts as "Canadian culture."

What is so interesting about these books is the way in which they both grapple specifically with Canadian programming, Hogarth with documentary television as a distinct genre, Tinic with Vancouver-based dramatic programs such as *X-Files*, an American network show, and *Da Vinci's Inquest*, one of the CBC's rare popular successes. This is a decid-edly new turn in Canadian television studies, a field that has tended to focus less on cultural production *per se* and more on telecommuni-cations and broadcasting policy. The leaders in this field are no doubt Marc Raboy and Robert Babe. Raboy's *Missed Opportunities: The Story of Canada's Broadcasting Policy* (1990), and Babe's *Telecommunications in Canada: Technology, Industry and Government* (1990) both lead from the scholars' long-standing – not to mention ongoing – public policy work for governmental and non-governmental agencies. In fact, it is worth pointing out that Raboy, along with David Taras, was the leading research consultant on *Our Cultural Sovereignty*.

More often than not, television is incorporated as one or two chapters in an anthology about Canadian media and culture. In recent years, there has been a noteworthy and long overdue expansion of this field. *The Cultural Industries in Canada* (1996), edited by Michael Dorland, awakened a renewed interest in the status of Canadian media, culture, communications technology, and the policy framework in which they all operate. An argument can be made that its successors in the field are *Mediascapes* (2002), edited by Paul Attallah and Leslie Shade, and *How Canadians Communicate* (2003), edited by David Taras, Frits Pannekoek, and Maria Bakardjieva. These books bring together scholars to discuss different forms of media and culture in order to suggest how they work collectively to shape a sense of national identity. While collections such as these play a crucial role in highlighting distinct aspects of Canadian media and their role in developing a coherent sense of Canadian culture, television merits additional close scrutiny as it bridges the major debates in the field, including technological and economic convergence, nationalism, and cultural value. It also provides key historical and political frameworks that are not always as readily obvious in other areas.

The value of these anthologies and textbooks on Canadian media resides in the way that they have rekindled debates about the role of media in shaping national identity. Additionally, the most recent of these books have highlighted just how unstable the idea of national identity truly is. However, these works often tend to emphasize technological or economic issues as if Canadian culture is simply a by-product of these larger structures. For that reason, we welcome another body of literature that more directly addresses cultural concerns. Books like Eva Mackey's *House of Difference* (1999) and Erin Manning's *Ephemeral Territories* (2003) directly address the idea of Canada as territory, nation, culture, and state. Mackey uses empirical and ethnographic evidence in order to reveal generations of marginalization and de-politicization for cultural and ethnic minorities, thereby challenging the cherished ideal of Canada as a multicultural nation defined by tolerance. Manning deconstructs the language of nationalism and its attachment to territorialism, the physical manifestation of what is fundamentally a discursive entity. These books point to new directions in Canadian cultural discourse that do not start with the assumption that Canada is a nation deserving of its own unique, identifiable culture, but which demonstrate that such a desire is itself at the heart of a deeply contradictory and ambivalent notion of nationalism that has serious repercussions for a nation's racial, linguistic, and ethnic "others."

These themes of ambivalence, deconstruction, ephemerality, and difference are indebted to the work of Linda Hutcheon and her landmark book *The Canadian Postmodern* (1988). She argues that, as a country obsessed with its borders, Canada is already operating within a quintessentially postmodern framework. She contests the modernist fixation of the nation-state as a site of unity, order, and rationality, suggesting on the contrary that, on aesthetic grounds, Canadian culture bypassed its modernist moment in order to arrive at a place where postmodern values have the upper hand. As she writes, "To render the particular concrete, to glory in a (defining) local ex-centricity – this is the Canadian postmodern" (19). This is, of course, a rather optimistic – and some may say naïve – conclusion to draw from Canada's policies of multiculturalism and continuing anxieties over regionalism. It reflects less the experience of ethnic communities and more the official stance of government on diversity, and a smug belief that the Canadian approach to the management of cultural difference is the best in the world. As the Canadian government's website on multiculturalism pronounces, "The Canadian experience has shown that multiculturalism encourages racial and ethnic harmony and cross-cultural understanding, and discourages ghettoization, hatred, discrimination and violence" (Canadian Heritage 2005). The notion that these social problems, which are offshoots of political and economic disenfranchisement, can be solved culturally through heritage programs and the like is precisely what authors like Mackey and Manning criticize.

Others, like Michael Dorland and Maurice Charland (2002), have countered Hutcheon's claims for postmodernism by arguing that Canada's ambivalence is more like an anxious looking back at missed opportunities than a progressive gaze forward to new potentialities.

Rather than having skipped modernism and moved directly onto post-modernism, Dorland and Charland argue that Canada is a country still in search of its modernist moment of nationalist certainty. They suggest that the forms of symbolic disruption that some identify as post-modern ruptures into the metanarratives of modernity and the unity of the sovereign nation-state are equally tied to political and economic forces of globalization that cannot be stopped by territorial borders (22). Their argument stems from their interest in Canadian civil and legal culture, not in the literary or artistic concerns of Hutcheon. Television, we argue, connects these two positions because it is a form of culture that is highly regulated by the state.

What Dorland and Charland define as Canadian "kynicism" (313), an ironic and reflexive sense of detachment from the ongoing search for an integral national identity, is, as Will Straw suggests, more common to English Canada than Quebec (2002, 96). Indeed, it should be stated quite clearly that it is difficult if not altogether impossible to discuss the situation of Canadian television without separating out the Quebec experience. Unlike the rest of Canada, where audiences for indigenous Canadian programming are consistently small and where the debates about identity are usually framed around the question of whether one exists at all much less how it would be defined, Québécois television is a vibrant but somewhat insulated cultural industry. Furthermore, its cultural distinctiveness from English Canada rests on linguistic, historical, and political grounds that have given that province a far greater sense of a unique and cohesive identity. Thus, while we are for the most part only interested in exploring the case of English language television culture in Canada, the example of Quebec is useful for delineating certain complex ideas around nations, states, and sovereign cultures.

The relationship between nation/state/culture is the major theme of the book. Following closely on that idea is the remapping of multiculturalism in the wake of globalization, which is forcing a major reevaluation of the very ideas of nations and states. Television as a medium comes more clearly into focus with our third theme of cultural value. As a mass medium and one that has been historically criticized as a debased form of culture, television is often cited as "lowbrow."

However, it is also a major tool in seemingly endless debates around national culture, particularly those that support protectionist policies. Thus, the value of television migrates along the high/low continuum depending on how it is being discussed, used, and evaluated. Finally, we look even more closely at the example of television as it mutates into a very different medium through changes in its technological and economic structure. These four themes of nation/state/culture, multiculturalism/globalization, high/low, and technological flows can perhaps be neatly framed within larger questions about modernity as opposed to postmodernity. They point to the way that the aesthetic and political value of television as a form of culture has been complicated by its technological and economic value as a form of mass media. At stake then, is a re-evaluation of Canada communication networks and their role in disseminating new forms of identity that can either better approximate or undo altogether the promise of enlightenment goals of tolerance, acceptance, and equality for all. This book is about television first and foremost, but it is also about notions of cultural citizenship and how television can help us to understand our place in national and global mediascapes.

NATION/STATE/CULTURE

The dialectic between nation and state is keenly felt in Canada since it is a country rife with regional tensions, an often-distorted sense of history that relies heavily on geography, and a future strongly linked to immigration. Nonetheless, there is no question that Canada is a sovereign state. We have an autonomous government, an official constitution, and a defined electoral system. We govern according to our own set of laws and accord citizenship to those who are either born here or have passed certain criteria and are committed to making Canada their home, all the things which define state sovereignty. However, it

is not as clear that Canada is a nation. By this, we mean a cultural entity that can clearly define itself and assert conditions of membership
based on shared experiences, values, language, and the like. This distinction is not merely semantic, but addresses the idea of the nation
as a cultural construct separate from the political or economic structure of the state. The relationship is easier to understand with regard
to Quebec. Through its sovereignty movement, Quebec can be seen as
a nation struggling to establish statehood by gaining full political and
economic control over its territorial boundaries. In contrast, Canada's
borders are not challenged by external forces. Nonetheless, Canadian
territorialism is challenged internally by the myriad groups who live
within the country but who do not share a single cohesive culture.
This is by no means a unique situation for Canada. If anything, the
Canadian identity crisis at least has the value of openly acknowledg-
ing that cultural cohesion is less a reality than a desire by the state
to demonstrate its legitimacy. Indeed, cultural strategies of control
are far more likely in democratic states where political and economic
options of coercion or outright force are no longer legitimate (Straw
2002, 98). The double bind of culture as both a strategy of cohesion
and its greatest threat lies at the heart of the decoupling of nation from
state. Traditional heritage politics have sought to artificially encapsu-
late, and therefore preserve, the marginality of other distinct cultures
within the discursive borders of a state. This is what Arjun Appadurai
means when he talks about how states work to "monopolize the moral
resources of community" (1990, 304). It's a policy by which the doors
to other cultures are opened, but not so widely so as they could over-
whelm the dominant culture.

Of course, this idea becomes problematic when the so-called dominant culture is as poorly defined and transitory as is Canada's. As a
colonial territory of Britain that only recently (in global geopolitical
terms) shook off that yoke, Canada came late to the nation-building
game. Furthermore, unlike other former British colonies like India
or the United States, it asserted its independence without a revolution around which its citizens could rally. This is an age-old argument about Canada that Dorland and Charland characterize as one
of both counter-revolution and "ressentiment" (2002, 19). A marked

inferiority complex and perpetual looking up to Britain for approval characterized the early stages of culture building in Canada in the nineteenth and early twentieth centuries. However, as new cultural technologies boomed and mass media were seen to be replacing both the high culture forms of the elite and more rural-based folk culture, Canada's cultural sector became increasingly subjugated by that of the United States. Policies in both television and film ensured open access for American product and curtailed Canada's own cultural activity. What we lacked in Canadian content, however, was more than made up for by decades of rampant communication network building. Thus, the goal of creating a sense of cohesion from sea to sea to sea was met originally and almost exclusively by technological expansion, with very little concomitant initiatives to provide indigenous cultural content. Maurice Charland has termed this "technological nationalism," defined through three contradictory stances. First is the use of technological infrastructure – such as the Canadian Pacific Railway or the CBC – to define nodal points of identity formation. Second is our angst-ridden dependency on foreign markets, a throwback to the idea of Canada as physically and culturally peripheral. Finally and related, the cultural imperative of Canada becomes technology itself with little in the way of actual content or production (2004, 36). As Canada's geographic territory opened up to the north and west, scattering isolated populations across the map, this lack of cultural content in favour of cultural pathways gave immigrant communities the opportunity to maintain a stronger link to their heritage, laying the foundation for multiculturalism, which became an official federal act in 1985.

Despite the fact that Canada has one of the most open and sophisticated telecommunication systems in the world, broadcasting has remained a central political concern for the creation and maintenance of a distinct Canadian culture. While no small amount of ink has been spent in debating the significance of a distinct national culture, in practice very little has been done to achieve it. Straw characterizes this as a form of "ethical incompleteness" (2002, 96) that marks English Canada in particular. It reflects a kind of liar's game in which citizens affirm their support for Canadian culture, whatever that may be, even as they somewhat guiltily continue to reject indigenous offerings in favour of imported culture, most notably from the United States. Television is probably the most visible example of this attitude. It's the sort of mindset that allows shows like *Canadian Idol* to be hailed as a success, even though it is clearly a knock-off of its even more successful American counterpart. It is a longstanding dilemma with which policy makers and cultural nationalists must regularly contend. Organizations like the Friends of Canadian Broadcasting, a non-profit group that advocates for Canadian content on radio and television and limits on foreign programming, clearly puts ethical concerns of national cohesion ahead of economic priorities. As they state in their goals, "Seeing who we are, how we feel and what we believe is a task worth the investment. It is also a task best met by Canadians" (Friends of Canadian Broadcasting 2005). On the other side of this debate are private broadcasters whose programming goals are more market-driven. However, it would not be fair to say that these private broadcasters are necessarily at odds with cultural nationalists, as they too argue for governmental measures that protect their rights over the broadcasting system to ensure Canadian ownership. To them, it doesn't matter which *Idol* you watch, so long as you watch it on a Canadian-owned station. Either way, both sides rely on a kind of nebulous invocation of "Canadianness" that continues to be defined within a very narrow, anglocentric framework reflecting our colonial legacy.

MULTICULTURALISM MEETS GLOBALIZATION

When pushed to define what distinguishes Canada from other nations, a common tendency is to point to multiculturalism, a policy of inclusion and tolerance where individuals may express multiple aspects of their cultural heritage freely without loss of a sense of identity. As the former prime minister and chief proponent of multiculturalism, Pierre Trudeau, suggested, national identity and cultural identity need not necessarily be coupled. Thus, a person could consider themselves a Canadian on national terms, but culturally could be many kinds of "hyphenated," cultural Canadian: Native-, French-, Indo-, Chinese-, and so on (Collins 1990, 26). Thus, just as nationhood and statehood are not necessarily conjoined, neither are nationality and cultural identity. Of course, the obvious assumption within this argument isn't that state, nation, and culture are equally valued, but in fact that cultural identity is subservient to national identity. It is this conceit of multiculturalism that allows Canada to present a nationalist myth of tolerance and acceptance of clearly identified "others" even as its cultural policies whitewash the very significant differences between those cultures and between them and a predominantly Anglo-European definition of Canadianness.

The arguments for a distinctly Canadian television culture, which is usually defined simply as one free of American influence, tend to follow on the heels of the multicultural defence of Canada. Canada is not a melting pot, say some, but a cultural mosaic. Despite recent data that indicates that Canadians are less likely to actually support the ideals of the cultural mosaic than are our neighbours to the south (Den Tandt 2005), it is a common assumption that there is room in our society for all forms of cultural expression – as long as they are secured under the common rubric of Canadianness. Of course, the problem is that there is no consensus on what that common rubric is or if it even exists at all. "Canadianness" is, in fact, one of the least understood and least clearly articulated concepts in the nation's lexicon. The result is a kind of reluctantly guilty commitment to a notion of Canadian culture in theory, but not in practice. However, this lack of commitment is not necessarily a problem. Indeed, it may well be the logical outcome of ongoing shifts in the relationship between culture, politics, and economics. Increasingly, cultural policy is pulled in two directions at once, creating a schism. On the one hand, the communications infrastructure – networks, technology, systems, and the like – is the stuff of economics, industry, investment, and development. Culture, on the other hand, to the extent that it is managed by the state, is there to shore up a sense of nationalist identity that serves in turn as the primary defence of the continuation of the state (Straw 2002, 98). In

Canada, this defence is built around the conception of culture through multiculturalism as a distinctly modern, progressive form of nation-building. It is, as Charles Taylor argues, grounded in a two-fold belief in the dignity of persons and the privileging of the individual, both highly modern conceptions. However, this definition of the citizen clashes with the desire of any state to control its boundaries, both territorial and ephemeral (1992, 63).

If, as Eva Mackey argues, national identity is the fundamental form of modern subjectivity, then the logic of multiculturalism could be seen as contradictory. As the argument goes, modernity and nation-building are about the creation of homogeneous cultures, and the erasure of difference. However, Mackey and others point out that nation-building is not only about homogeneity, but also about plurality, and the creation of a consensus-based public in which limited levels of diversity are tolerated and made ancillary to a core identity (1999, 5). In that sense, then, multiculturalism can be regarded as a rather ingenious form of hegemony from within. Ultimately, the defining motif of Canadianness has to be acknowledged as ill-defined. Canadian identity is more clearly a strategy that distinguishes Canada from the national identities of other nations than it is a confident statement of identity. Canada is defined in the abstract as something that the United States, to take the most common comparison, is not: *we* are a mosaic, *they* are a melting pot. The "they" barely needs to be mentioned by name, of course, while the "we" remains rather nebulous. The anxiety over American influence is so keenly felt in Canada that it circumscribes nearly every facet of national cultural policy. In particular, this anxiety defines Canadian television, and it has only increased as technological, economic, and political barriers crumble in the wake of globalization.

As an important paradigm for conceptualizing culture and communication at the current moment, globalization can mean many things. Opponents see it as a nefarious strategy of worldwide homogenization or, more starkly, the Americanization of global cultures. Others see potential in opening up communicative pathways between marginalized or heretofore silenced groups and creating new forms of imagined communities across territories. We are not taking part in this particular debate, as we recognize that both tendencies operate simultaneously in the way that television is produced, disseminated, and understood. In this sense, television is a critical site for exploring the limits of globalization because it operates across so many different geographies. There is the physical or territorial location, in which broadcasting is a major concern of the state and subject to stringent regulation. There is also the virtual or symbolic geography, in which television flows across physical boundaries and connects audiences to networks of identity that transcend the nation-state (Tinic 2005, 17). Furthermore, television straddles both the public and private spheres. It is on the one hand a crucial instrument of nationalism and public identity formation, while on the other a distinctly private practice undertaken in isolation by atomized audiences who need neither be citizens of the nation nor located within its boundaries (Gripsrud 2004, 212).

In the rush to claim a collapse of boundaries and a new era of free-flowing goods, people, information, and culture, the concept of globalization falters in that it overlooks its connection to nationalism. Rather than see it as supplanting an obsolete, static mode of identity formation, we agree with scholars such as David Morley (2000) and Serra Tinic (2005) in seeing globalization as a new focal point through which to articulate the legitimacy of the nation-state. Television makes this clear in that globalization has been used to justify tearing down regulatory boundaries and untying broadcasting from its nationalist moorings. At the same time, cultural content regulations continue to proliferate to ensure that programming reflects some kind of bounded notion of community and identity and protects the nation from the homogenizing effects of globalization. What is interesting is the way in which both invoke a spectre of the global as the foe of the nation-state and insist upon a decidedly liberal notion of the public sphere grounded in free markets, consumer choice, and individualism. We reject this definition but continue to explore the potential of a globalization that doesn't merely skip over the national to get to the local, but works dialectically across the terrain in order to reveal more nuanced, pluralistic, and democratic forms of nationalism built on multiplicity and difference, in the spirit of multiculturalism.

For Canada, the anxieties now being produced worldwide by globalization have circulated in other forms for generations. As Canadian
communication scholars have long pointed out, Canada has been ex-
emplary in creating vast communication infrastructures necessary for
linking the country to itself, from the railroads to the CBC to new initiatives in the "Supernet." In many ways, communication systems are
the precursors of globalization, ignoring as they do any kind of physical, territorial borders (Collins 1990, 9). The ability of communication
systems to dissolve territoriality highlights an interesting aspect of the
problem of nationhood. Space, place, and location begin to mean very
different things once they can be transcended altogether. Manning argues in her analysis of Canadian identity politics that territorialism
isn't as much a physical phenomenon as it is a discursive entity. By
that she means that the physical space of Canada only becomes meaningful when it is understood as the foundation for a sense of place.
We come to an understanding of what Canada means by translating
our surroundings into something meaningful that shapes our relationship to others. Canada, a rural-based, staples economy for so long,
has emphasized this sense of space/place in its nationalist metaphors,
from the beaver to the maple leaf and our own slogan, "from sea to sea
to sea." The rural Canadian mythology is so ingrained that, in 2004,
when Statistics Canada announced what everyone already knew, that
the country had become a predominantly urban society, it made head-
lines across the country. The geographical landscape of this country is
changing dramatically, while the real battleground remains the discursive landscape of an imagined Canada, a nation rhetorically committed to tolerance, openness, and respect for others.

If multiculturalism really did mean what its proponents say it does,
then Canada would be well poised to embrace globalization. However,
as trends in television show, the tendency is to look for ways to shore
up resistance to globalization in order to create the conditions for the
impossible dream of a one-way flow of Canadian cultural goods to the
world. Part of the project of this book, then, is to imagine a different
kind of multiculturalism that also re-imagines globalization beyond
the parameters of the liberal public sphere. The dominant form of multiculturalism has tended toward a homogenization of non-dominant

cultures to the point where they can be reduced to colourful costumes, spicy food, and an annual street festival. In that sense, they remain resolutely "othered," de-politicized and asked to feel grateful that they are allowed to maintain any sense of hybrid identity at all. Taking as our starting point the groundbreaking ideas of Arjun Appadurai, we wonder what are the possibilities of understanding hyphenated Canadianness not as a form of conjuncture, of erasure of differences, but of disjuncture.

In brief, Appadurai argues that anxieties that globalization will herald homogenization, commodification, or the outright Americanization of culture neglect to note the complexity by which territorialism is giving way to deterritorialism, or the dissolution of borders between sovereign states. In this sense, he suggests that the relationship between the nation and the state is becoming an increasingly unstable one, threatening to break the other apart rather than maintaining a solid centre (1990, 304). At the heart of this deterritorialization are two new forms of landscape, the mediascape, or the free-flow of images and texts that eventually cohere into narratives of identity and location, and the ideoscape, a concatenation of ideas and political beliefs that alter the definition of the state. Together, they, along with the rapid flows of money (finanscapes), networks (technoscapes) and people (ethnoscapes), make possible new territories for cultural infiltration. The results can be either inward or outward looking. In the former, an increased sense of nationalism, distinguished from one's statehood, makes the qualifier in hyphenated identities more powerful. Similarly, those who remain committed to a state-based sense of identity could be inclined to police the boundaries of nationalism and keep it contained from political influence. Some could argue this has been the tendency of Canadian multiculturalism in its most liberal, nationalist form. Yet, on the other hand, Appadurai suggests that as globalization accelerates the pace of disjuncture between media, ideas, money, technology, and people, new alternatives arise. Rather than fearing this sense of deterritorialization, we can look out onto new landscapes in which disjuncture and difference are not problems to be fixed, but promises to be fulfilled. The mediascape is leading the way, he says, by creating new markets for culture that satisfy the desires of diasporic

populations to maintain a connection to the places that they left behind (1990, 303). As a country based on immigration, Canada is well
situated to play a significant role in the globalizing mediascape, but
only if it is willing to let go its dreams of unified nationhood in order to
embrace the new alternatives provided by genuine multiculturalism.

TELEVISION AND ITS AUDIENCES

Television has occupied a space at the centre of debates over globalization, nationalism, and multiculturalism since it was first launched in
Canada. It is still the most powerful form of mass media, and certainly
the one that penetrates into the highest number of Canadian homes.
Yet, television also suffers from a longstanding feeling of debasement.
It has been marginalized and degraded by the belief that it is a low
form of culture pandering to the worst kind of taste. Interestingly,
that has led to a tension between what the medium is and what many
wish that it could become within the context of Canadian nationalism.
More than any other cultural form, Canadian television is claimed as
the lifeline to the hearts and minds of the nation's people. It can either
pump in the kinds of values that will sustain the nation as a whole, or it
will clog our national arteries with seductive content from elsewhere.
As a result, television is one of the most regulated media and has been
the subject of a seemingly endless number of governmental studies,
commissions, and hearings. The crux of the problem – at least to those
who continue to see it as such – is that by and large, Canadians in overwhelming numbers watch American programming more than home-
grown fare. For this reason, the debate over television in Canada has
tended to be shaped by the perceived threat of the United States and
its globalizing homogenization, and also by the notion that American
programming is a cheap succour for passive audiences who simply
won't watch what's good for them.

As we have noted, Canada's attempts at creating a cohesive national identity tend to work within strategies of distinction rather than definition. Nowhere is this more apparent than in the relationship to American culture. Straw characterizes the two main thrusts of this defence against Americanism as essentialist and compensatory. The essentialist model, which valiantly struggles to produce a list of universal characteristics that succinctly and definitively create the essence of Canada, is rapidly losing ground in the wake of increasing multiculturalism (2002, 103). The compensatory model is a much more interesting argument. It simply states that what Canadian culture most often provides are those things that other cultures do not. Rather than competing directly with expensive American network dramatic programming, Canadian television offers audiences the stuff that its more commercial counterpart does not provide; in this instance, a tasteful, low-key version of television better suited to the genteel mentality of Canada (2002, 106). From this standpoint, Canadian identity is defined by a fervent desire to be not-American, and this sensibility fuels much of the cultural policy that currently defines television in this country. In this sense, television is made doubly low. First, by its connection to a nation that is seen as the arbiter of all things crass, tacky, and overblown. Second, by its status as a mass medium that strives for popularity over edification. The goal, for cultural nationalists, has long been to raise the stature of television by ensuring that it is provided with content that is more in keeping with the aesthetic and nationalist values of Canada.

Richard Collins defines this as the Beethoven versus Aaron Spelling dilemma and notes that much of the anxiety surrounding mass media has to do with the idea of taking the internationalism of culture out of the hands of the elite (1990, 26). One does not worry about the homogenizing influence of Beethoven because his works are regarded as canonical and uplifting, while those of Spelling, the producer of programs such as *Charlie's Angels*, *Dynasty*, and *Beverly Hills 90210*, are condemned as deadeningly commercial. The class privilege delineated by a cosmopolitanism that can be had only by those who can speak other languages, appreciate other cultures, and travel to other countries has, in recent years, been usurped by the ethnoscape of

immigrants and migatory labourers, substituting, in the minds of conservative commentators, bad forms of globalized popular culture for
good forms of elite culture. The fear of these new roving Others is, ironically, made acute not by the culture they import with them – which
is actually quite tightly controlled and limited in Canada – but by the
threat of cultural assimilation that they pose through the ubiquitous-
ness of American programming. From the point of view of Canadian
nationalism, the concern is that the newly arriving multicultural
masses will not properly assimilate as hyphenated Canadians, but
rather will help to speed the death of Canadian programming on the
airwaves by assimilating to the wrong culture, or by failing to appreciate the subtle distinctions between America's *Entertainment Tonight*
and Canada's *eTalk Daily*.

The key strategy of a distinctly Canadian television culture can be
defined as one of middleness. Canadian television cannot be highbrow
because those pretensions threaten to alienate the very audiences that
nationalists seek to enlighten and bring into the fold. To create difficult
programming would be in opposition to the values of multiculturalism, where plurality, democracy, and tolerance are at a premium. At
the same time, Canadian television cannot be low, because that is the
position that we have ceded to the Americans, and the occupation of
this position would fail to sufficiently distinguish Canada from the culture of the United States. Thus, Canadian television achieves a middle
position primarily through its definition of itself as neither/nor.

However, in striving for the open-minded middle, Canadian television seeks to produce that middleness through a rhetoric of choice.
As Appadurai notes, the commercialization of values like plurality and
diversity in the mediascape has undermined political agency and replaced it with liberal notions of personal choice (1990, 307). Thus, even
as Canada invokes protectionist measures to ensure a strong media
sector by keeping foreign broadcasters from broadcasting in this country, the country remains one of the most diverse and open television
markets in the world. In addition to nearly all that American television
has to offer, there is also Canadian programming, specialty channels,
subscription services, and more. Thanks in part to decades of infrastructure building, Canada is in a state of highly advanced and

expansive television abundance. Yet, this abundance is of a single type. If there is any area where the country fails to deliver, it is in providing a full range of multicultural programming options. Foreign language services (in Canada, that means other than French or English) are as limited on television as they are elsewhere in the culture, and significantly trail the options available in many other countries. Canadian television, therefore, does not work to disseminate difference so much as to repatriate it. When notions of plurality and difference become part of the hegemonic system of state control over national identity, they are revealed to be little more than commodities to be deployed in the interest of the governing and the industry elite. In other words, fear of homogenization from our neighbour to the south helps support cultural policies that allow for a more subtle form of homogenization from within (Apparadurai 1990, 307). Television, with its promises of attaining a pure expression of middleness, is a chief tool in this strategy.

REDIRECTING THE FLOW

Ever since cultural theorist Raymond Williams spent a lonely night in a Miami hotel room watching American television, no metaphor has been used as thoroughly to define the televisual experience as "flow" (Williams 1989). Now, in the era of globalization where everything from money to people to ideas is seen to be in constant motion, there seems little reason to abandon the term. However, as the traditional north-south axis of encroaching Americanism is increasingly revealed to be an outmoded way of conceptualizing flow, it is necessary to reconsider the term within the wider currents of global scapes. The signs of this change appear everywhere. Debates now rage over the potential of converging media forms as technologies flow into one another, driven by massive capital ventures and international conglomerates.

The promises of interactive WebTV or downloadable "slivercasts" raise the possibility of dramatically altering how we watch and even use the television. It is not altogether clear that in the future television will remain as a distinct medium of broadcasting. Yet, as many critics point out, these futuristic directions often neglect the value of television as a domestic-based medium that provides information and entertainment in a wide range of forms at the touch of a button. For many writers and critics, it is necessary to shift television to something that it is not in order to raise it from its status as low culture. We are not those critics. It is our belief that television, for the foreseeable future, will retain its dominant position even as the medium morphs along with the new flow.

The ideology of need, Williams notes, fuels much of the debate around the future of television. This is a relatively simple but vitally important belief that technology does not create culture, but rather that culture creates technologies. It is an important idea, given Canada's own intellectual history of technological determinism and our public policy of building ever more expanding communications networks while paying lip service to what they will carry. Rather than suggesting that Canada has been sitting back passively amidst the onslaught of technological progress, we argue that the present shape and future direction of Canadian television is the result of a longstanding and deliberate strategy that has elevated some technologies over others based on the ideological infrastructure of multiculturalism, plurality, and diversity which has taken its most liberal form as "personal choice."

Thus, part of the polemic of this book is to call for a redirection of flows. This occurs in three ways. First, a move away from our longstanding obsession with the threat of American assimilation and toward a more global outlook in which we open up television to increased foreign language and cultural content. Second, a shift from an understanding of multiculturalism as a form of pseudo-benign paternalism in which other cultures are rendered quaint or are kept resolutely marginalized from the inner circles of political power, and toward a more materially grounded form of multiculturalism that insists on giving ground to the margins and questioning the very need for a central vision of Canadianness that would trump all other nationalisms. Third, we challenge the tendency under which economic and technological issues have dominated television policy, in favour of placing greater emphasis on the idea of the audience and television as a cultural form; and, in so doing, emphasizing the potential of television as a decidedly public experience. It is in this last point that we consider television to still be of vital importance not only in media and cultural debates but in discussions about the flow of world order on national, global, and local scales. Television, a modern visual spectacle, is one of the key sites for the sorts of symbolic disruption that coincide with massive shifts in the movement of political and economic capital. Its existence is predicated on the values of consumption, not reason. These values have traditionally provided a backdoor entrance for marginalized people into the public sphere (Warner 1994, 397). The goal here, then, is to use the example of Canadian television in order to re-imagine its potential as a form of communicative action, a key player in the symbolic lifeworld of any society. That may be asking too much, as the commodified status of the medium could prove to be a formidable barrier to a radically democratized transformation. Nonetheless, the breaking down of the myths of Canadian television as a perpetual victim of forces beyond the nation's control that leaves it struggling for survival can in turn open up new ways of thinking about nationalism altogether, particularly its increasingly antagonistic relationship to the mediascape.

In the chapters that follow, we examine the state of contemporary Canadian television in order to reveal certain critical disjunctures between the ideals and practices of industry, government, artists, and audiences. In chapter one, "Regulation," the current normative framework for television is laid out. The major stakeholders in the cultural field from the political, economic, and cultural sectors are identified: broadcasters, cable companies, and cultural producers on the one hand; political commissions, regulatory agencies, and lobbying groups on the other. It is the intersecting interests of these two sets of players that are primarily responsible for the shape of Canadian television as it exists today, and the framework in which regulation is negotiated. Two key, interrelated tensions frame the regulatory debates over television, which in the broadest terms can be defined as cultural and economic imperatives. The separation of these imperatives is muddied by Canada's own quasi-public broadcasting system that includes both a revenue-driven public network and fully private networks that are monitored by the Canadian Radio-television and Telecommunication Commission (CRTC), which is ultimately answerable to the federal government. Examples from European and community broadcasting highlight the contradictory status of Canadian television vis-à-vis other forms of programming and regulation. Other government initiatives to increase and improve the standing of Canadian programming, either through Canadian Content regulations or through the allocation of public funds for program creation, as with the Canadian Television Fund (CTF), ensure that television is always on the governmental agenda. However, the cultural and the economic functions of television were severed from each other in the 1990s by the business-oriented politics of Brian Mulroney's Conservative government, leading to an artificial divide that allows the media industry to proceed according to capital-driven goals while shoring up support for its private initiatives through hollow invocations for the need to guarantee Canadian culture primarily through the protection of private ownership.

Chapter two, "Programming," does something that very few works on Canadian television have done: actually consider what's on. While the dismissal of most Canadian television programming by audiences as low-rent Americanism or pious nationalist posturing does, historically and unfortunately, have some basis in truth, there are some provocative examples that both support and belie this attitude. The underlying anxieties over television's status as a lowbrow medium and the need to posit Canada as America's middlebrow other have led to some very interesting strategies in the development of Canadian programming. The most important relationship is between informational and entertainment programming. While Canada is widely held to have excelled at the former, the country is in a never-ending crisis regarding the latter. Nonetheless, there are a number of programs worth investigating in some depth. *Canadian Idol*, the knock-off of the American knock-off of the UK's *Pop Idol*, has been hailed as a tremendous lowbrow commercial success, one of the first times that a Canadian show other than hockey has topped the ratings in recent memory. By contrast, the sitcom *Corner Gas* strives for a distinct form of Canadianicity with its low-key comedic stylings, its use of well-loved Canadian television and theatre stars from the past, and its setting in rural Saskatchewan. Consistently reaching the lower ranks of the top twenty shows, it is one of the highest rated English-Canadian dramatic programs in recent history. Perhaps the single most successful Canadian television series is an internationally recognized franchise. *Degrassi*, which is currently in its fourth incarnation, has slowly evolved into cult-like status. Originally launched by the CBC but now taken up by CTV, the program represents an international dramatic success story unlike anything that the public broadcaster has been able to come up with in a generation. Instead, the CBC has increasingly turned to the reality market by poaching British television in an effort to create a water cooler show. *The Greatest Canadian* is a reality-based show in which Canadian public figures (it would be too great a stretch to call them celebrities) vie for the right to have their candidate elected the greatest Canadian. In many ways, the show represents the worst kind of nationalist pandering. Yet, the structure of the program, its use of well-known Canadian faces from film, television, sports, and even politics, and the ready support lent to it by other media says something about the power of television to act as a forum for nationalism in the face of globalization.

Finally, in chapter three, "Technology," we explore the delivery system itself in order to understand why some innovations are being hotly debated while others are barely even acknowledged. The face of television is changing from the classical model in which images flow from the screen to a mass audience. In its place is a model that finds the flow originating with the audience itself, as they deftly manipulate the fullest limits of the medium and adapt it to their needs. Yet, despite the fact that the country has invested in some of the most sophisticated technological systems possible, Canada is beginning to lag behind other countries as it insists on defining its technological needs based on ideologies of victimization and survival against the American media juggernaut. We look at three technologies that we feel are dramatically restructuring the way that television is experienced: DVD releases of television shows; digital video recorders that allow audiences to time-shift television according to their own schedules;

and peer-to-peer file-sharing networks that make it possible to download television shows after they've aired. Finally, we explore one technology that is being hotly debated even though its impact will not be anywhere near as keenly felt as the other three: HDTV. High definition television is dominating debate within industry and the CRTC, driven by the fear of American networks outpacing Canadians, while the very structure of the industry is being called into question by new delivery systems.

This is a book that deals with three broad areas of interest: the technology of television, the people who watch it and the programs that they watch, and the regulatory framework that exists in Canada to mediate between the two. At stake, then, in examining television is an understanding of how Canada can accommodate massive shifts in the global technoscape, ethnoscape, finanscape, ideoscape, and crucially, the mediascape. In that sense, television becomes a crucial nexus around which larger issues about national identity, globalization, cultural sovereignty, the spaces of public discourse, and technological dominance are unravelled. It is clear to us that the technological shifts of the past several years – and the coming years – have thrown the issue of what television is and what it could be very much into doubt. Similarly, the changing face of Canada as a nation through immigration, urbanization, and globalization has placed the issue of national identity firmly at centre stage once again. While early evidence about changing experiences of television viewing may hint at the future, we do not know with precise certainty how the existing television technologies will change viewer expectations and uses, nor how newer technologies will rewrite the rules of television. What we do know, however, is that the game is in the process of changing, for better or worse. Likewise, we do not how Canada will continue to grow as a nation in the coming years. We cannot predict the changes that the country will undergo, nor the political choices that will be made by its citizens. What we can do, however, is to look closely and specifically at where we are now, and determine what the state of Canadian television is at the moment. In so doing, we hope to diagnose some of the obvious failings of Canada's television policy in order to provide a better orientation toward an uncertain future.

CHAPTER ONE:

GULATION

I n June 2004, in the midst of a federal election campaign, the Conservative party and its leader, Stephen Harper, came under fire for their stance on broadcasting issues. Although the party's official party platform had no mention of broadcasting, briefing notes provided to Conservative candidates called for opening Canadian airwaves to competition from American satellite companies, reducing the power of the CRTC, and relaxing foreign ownership regulations for media ("Tories would" 2004). These revelations followed comments made by Harper in May in which he speculated about placing the CBC on a "more commercial" footing (Friesen 2004). Now in power with a minority government, the Conservatives immediately stepped up these moves, causing consternation on Parliament Hill for Canadian cultural and communications sovereignty (Curry 2006, B6). While these policy moves are well in keeping with the Tory economic platform that has long promoted privatization and fiscal responsibility, they are totally at odds with the traditional culturally based arguments for a protectionist, quasi-public broadcasting system. The federal government has played a central role in the history of Canadian television, not simply because of the funding that it provides to the CBC, and which the Tories implicitly threatened to reduce even more drastically after years of similar Liberal budget-slashing, but through the protections offered to private broadcasters by the CRTC. In questioning these protections, the Conservatives are being accused by NDP critics and others of threatening the entire broadcasting model, and with it the idea of Canadian cultural sovereignty altogether. To counter criticisms that they are in effect killing national broadcasting, party spokesperson Andrew Skaling framed the issue as a matter of choice. He said, "The reality is it's a 500-channel universe. It's a question of Canadians having choice as to what they want to watch." (Jack 2004). This invocation of the audience as the locus of their concerns failed to sway many commentators who observed that the proposals could "eliminate Canadian programming and make the broadcasters subsidiaries of American media giants" (Reguly 2004).

During the 2005 federal election that gave Harper's Tories a minority government, cultural issues received even less debate than they had the year previous. The Tory platform for culture and media highlights several ideological conflicts that have plagued Canadian television since the earliest days of broadcasting. The first is the opposition between Canadian and foreign (really, American) media interests. The second is the invocation of "choice," and its implied opposite, regulation, as marking a democratic, pluralistic broadcasting system. The third is the longstanding dilemma between public and private broadcasting in this country in which one network, the CBC, is effectively run on a hybrid model where it must simultaneously serve national interests as determined by the state and prove itself competitive with the private networks CTV and Global without relying (as its competitors do) on imported U.S. programs to inflate its ratings. And finally, there is the desire to somehow create a paternalistic policy for television that will reflect, if not outright enact, the principles of multiculturalism as they were enshrined in a parliamentary act since 1985. All these concerns have been invoked time and time again, particularly around moments of intense political upheaval like an election. The important thing about the Canadian experience, however, is the extent to which broadcasting is taken seriously as a national – and nationalist – concern. It is impossible to sever the development of television in this country from the expansion of the nation-state over the course of the twentieth century. The two are deeply enmeshed, as television has been an effective tool in cultural politics to justify the state through nationalist rhetoric and a claim to sovereign cultural identity.

A standard trope for analyzing Canadian broadcasting has been to look through the eyes of the government and regulatory agencies, rather than at the screen or to the audience. While we would prefer to avoid that route, it is nonetheless necessary to provide some background to the current state of the broadcasting debate in this country in order to move the discussion forward. In general, the path of Canadian television can be marked by six major federal reports, all known colloquially by the names of their chairs: Aird (1929), Massey-Levesque (1949–51), Fowler (1956–7), Applebaum-Hébert (1981–2), Caplan-Sauvageau (1986), and Lincoln (2003). The Aird Commission, formally known as the Royal Commission on Radio Broadcasting, is perhaps best known for establishing the framework that led to the founding of the Canadian Radio-Broadcasting Corporation, which later dropped the term *radio* in order to encompass all forms of broadcasting, and is commonly known as the CBC. The vision laid out by Aird was to place broadcasting in the service of the state in order to promote a nationalist spirit and spread the word of federalism at a time when this country was barely out of its colonial crib (Gasher 1997, 16).

The Aird vision was carried forward by the Royal Commission on National Development in the Arts, Letters and Sciences, or the Massey Commission, in establishing other federalist cultural organizations like the National Film Board, and strengthening the CBC. A goal of the Massey Commission was to create a strongly public, not private, infrastructure for culture and communication that would be directly monitored by Parliament. In general, the consensus is that Massey shored up the nationalist barricades in order to "protect the nation from excessive commercialization and Americanization" (in Gasher 1997, 19). While there is certainly some truth to that statement, recent revisionist history by scholars like Zoë Druick have highlighted the internationalist sentiment embedded in the final report. Druick notes that underlying the more obvious nationalist rhetoric was a concern to bring Canada onto an international stage and to support efforts by the newly formed United Nations to make culture a wide-sweeping political concern that would both strengthen sovereign countries and provide conduits toward greater cooperation on a global stage (Druick 2006). In many ways, then, what the Massey Commission did was to lay the foundations for both a publicly driven cultural sector based on the federalist ideal of the establishment of a uniquely Canadian

national character, and also for later developments in multiculturalism from a deliberately liberal perspective, that is one based on individualism, open markets, and freedom of choice.

Together, these two royal commissions laid a solid foundation
for an idea of broadcasting as a federal initiative committed to the
creation and maintenance of a shared sense of national identity and
unity. This belief was only strengthened by the avidly nationalistic
Royal Commission on Broadcasting, or the Fowler Commission, in
1956 (Gasher 1997, 23). Following it, the 1960s and 1970s were marked
by heady patriotism spearheaded by the long-serving prime minister,
Pierre Elliott Trudeau. In 1968, the Broadcasting Act came into law.
Importantly, its drafting was framed around distinctly nationalistic
ideals about how broadcasting should serve the cultural, social, and
economic infrastructure of the country. To that end, it not only enshrined the CBC as the national broadcaster and implemented protectionist measures for an indigenous production industry, it also created
a regulatory system that would maintain Canadian sovereignty over
the airwaves. The Canadian Radio-television Commission, renamed
in 1976 as the Canadian Radio-television and Telecommunications
Commission, was launched as part of the mandate of the Broadcasting
Act. Interestingly enough, despite the name change, the CRTC seems
not to have incorporated telecommunications into its nationalist agenda. On its website it states clearly that the purpose of Canadian broadcasting is to serve as "a tool for protecting and promoting Canadian
culture and achieving key social objectives. Legislators and regulatory
bodies in Canada have acknowledged that Canadian broadcasting is
essential to preserving our national sovereignty" (CRTC). However,
there are no such lofty ambitions for telecommunications. Thus, a divide between cultural and economic drivers appears to have been embedded in the CRTC from its outset.

In 1982 the Cultural Policy Review Committee, chaired by Louis
Applebaum and Jacques Hébert, detoured slightly from the cultural
nationalist path forged by the royal commissions that preceded it, first
by its refusal to invoke the spectre of American encroachment, and
second by accepting some degree of privatization as inevitable, especially now that television was the ascendant medium. In the 1980s, the

cold water of economic realities began to drown out the voices of hard-core federalism. Furthermore, regional divisions in the country began to show themselves more visibly, most noticeably in Quebec, which held its first sovereignty referendum in 1980. However, even in English Canada, the regions became increasingly critical of a highly centrist – or, to be more exact, Torontocentric – perspective that seemed to dominate the CBC. As Serra Tinic argues, as national broadcasting policy evolved, it mimicked longstanding economic relationships between centres and peripheries on both national and global scales. The interesting outcome is that those regions marginalized on a national scale have found new and better markets by entering into a global television economy, undermining nationalist rhetoric about the power of television to forge a distinct Canadian identity (2005, 4). Confronted with economic and political resistance to federalism's isolationist and paternalistic tendencies, the Applebaum-Hébert report embraced what would soon become the official federal policy of multiculturalism. It also softened the federal role in all forms of culture, encouraging the government to act as a facilitator for private enterprise (Gasher 1997, 25). That is not to say that the culturalists lost out completely to the economists, but that the arguments for national culture were softened in order to promote a more liberal economic agenda of choice, profit, and audience maximization.

Five years later the Caplan-Savageau Committee, officially the Task Force on Broadcasting Policy, tried to reinstate a protectionist model for national culture overseen by a benevolent but powerful state. By that time the Trudeau era had given way to a Conservative government headed by Brian Mulroney that famously sought closer ties to the United States and its own privatization agenda according to the principles of Reaganomics. Culture remained a passionately debated issue, especially during the protracted discussion that led to the Free Trade Agreement with the United States, and later the North American Free Trade Agreement with the United States and Mexico. However, there was more howling in the wilderness than actual exchange of ideas. Ironically, it can be argued that it was the values of multiculturalism that allowed culture to become a secondary concern and established the rhetoric of choice for justifying economic encroachment on cultural issues. Multiculturalism within a liberal framework claimed that Canadian citizens chose the particular configuration of their national identity, but not in a way that would directly impact on the state's fundamental identity. They were to do so through an invocation of their culture, divorced from a sense of politics or economics in such a way that turned history into the far less imposing idea of heritage. It is, therefore, not really a surprise that the federal Department of Communication was split in two by the mid-1990s so that communications networks fell under the jurisdiction of industry while a newly formed Department of Canadian Heritage took on the problems of culture as a separate concern. Form and content were effectively divorced from each other, but more importantly, culture was unmoored from the material conditions of its production and turned into little more than a nationalist form of piety. Heritage implies tradition and nostalgia, as if culture is something Canadians remember fondly from a time before more urgent concerns were pressed upon them.

In 2003, the first report on Canadian television in nearly twenty years was tabled by the House of Commons Standing Committee on Heritage, chaired by Clifford Lincoln. The interesting thing about this report is how much it was shaped by new technological and economic realities facing television, even though these telecommunication concerns are no longer a part of the jurisdiction of the Heritage Committee. At the turn of the century, the effects of cable, satellite, and digital technologies are beginning to be forcefully felt. However, what has also changed is the make-up of Canada, which is expanding through immigration, particularly from countries beyond Europe, including Africa, the Middle East, and South-East Asia. Interestingly, though, the final report did not directly address the changing ethnoscape of Canada beyond the usual platitudes regarding multiculturalism. Instead, it remained fixed on the technological and economic concerns for the Canadian television industry and the need to protect the industry from encroaching globalization. Two visions of television culture were presented as co-equivalents in the report. The first was a paternalistic claim to Canadian cultural sovereignty and the fostering of a distinct national identity that would best be realized through a strong, independent, mostly private media sector that is nonetheless sheltered from foreign competition and bolstered by national subsidy programs, with the CBC providing a kind of moral counterweight. The second was the call for diversity and plurality on the airwaves in the form of consumer choice through expanded communications systems, in particular digital cable and satellite convergence. What both of these value statements share at the core, and what makes them mutually supportive, is the fact that both are geared toward a very narrow idea of Canadian television within a North American market. Thus, they are based upon assumptions of dominant anglocentrism that sees globalization as a process of cultural and economic homogenization (i.e., Americanization) rather than as a set of multicultural disjunctures.

Unfortunately for the authors of the Lincoln report, no sooner had it been tabled than the 2004 election was called. While culture barely registered on the political charts, it did occasionally surface as when Stephen Harper publicly mused about undoing the federalist-public structure of broadcasting altogether. His party offered a very different vision of broadcasting than the dominant cultural rhetoric that was evident in the Lincoln report, stressing consumer choice and the elimination of the government's role in culture, highlighting competition and greater integration with the American marketplace. The platforms offered by the Liberals, New Democratic Party, and the Bloc Québécois were far more in line with the standard federalist position, each calling for a healthy cultural sector reliant on government intervention and subsidy. The fact that the cultural platforms of the Bloc, NDP, and Liberals are only marginally differentiated demonstrates the high degree of consensus that has been achieved around cultural issues in Canada. In effect, it seems to be agreed by everyone but the Conservative party that Canadian culture is a fragile thing to be nurtured by nationalist-driven policies that want to achieve a balance between popularity and profitability while reflecting a sense of common Canadianness defined in distinction to the dominant modes of culture produced by American broadcasting.

In this sense, it can be said that the health of Canadian culture is measured according to two very different criteria. The first, the economic yardstick, favours competitiveness, an open marketplace, and technological innovation. The profitability of the broadcasting sector is the key metric here. The second, the cultural yardstick, clings to a belief that culture can be somehow contained and artificially propped up under the guise of authentic national experience. The "quality," however defined, of the Canadian cultural experience is the gauge in this instance. The central issue is that both of these yardsticks take as their point of comparison the American cultural experience. In that sense, then, Canada is automatically set up for failure in the eyes of its own cultural mavens.

Television, as the most ubiquitous cultural medium, is emblematic of an anti-triumphalist discourse. Its cultural, economic, and techno-logical form makes the kind of gatekeeping that cultural elites pre-fer difficult. Television is a democratic mass medium, open and easily available to everyone in a variety of forms. In the private model of broadcasting, this results in a rhetoric of consumer choice based on ratings-driven programming. Public models are more concerned with providing access across the spectrum of populations, serving dispa-rate communities, and providing an array of images and narratives that everyone can cleave to as a nation. The Canadian system, how-ever, is almost an exact balance of these two very distinct models and is therefore caught in a schizophrenic position of serving opposing goals. Stakeholders in broadcasting have very different ideas about how to solve this dual dilemma of economic and cultural marginaliza-tion in their own country. Their battleground is the CRTC. It is before this commission that signal providers (cable and satellite companies), cultural producers, and networks battle to secure their own particular visions of Canadian television. The Canadian public plays a tangen-tial, but frequently invoked, role in these debates, framed as both con-sumers – most often defined around individual choice – and as citizens – defined through notions of common nationalist identity.

Of these stakeholder groups, the cable industry is the most closely aligned with the Conservative party's interest in consumer choice, al-though it would balk at increased competition from American signal providers. Its version of open markets extends only so far as its own ability to broadcast American channels on its systems to Canadians, but not so far as to allow Canadians direct access to American cable or satellite systems. Artists and television producers are quicker to embrace increased funding and tighter regulations on Canadian content, as these mean more jobs for Canadian cultural producers and more likelihood that their shows will be bought by Canadian networks. For their part, the broadcast networks range between the two poles, depending on the individual issue and their own particular financial stake in it. At the most basic level, of course, all three groups demand the same thing: more of what benefits their shareholders. While each frames their discussion in terms of what is best for Canadian viewers, self-interest is clearly the primary driver in any debate on the future of television. That, in and of itself, is not particularly revelatory. What is important is the way that individual stakeholder groups mobilize arguments in order to present their interests as equivalent to the interests of Canadians as citizens, and, further, how this self-presentation in turn frames the regulatory context for television in this country. By examining the way that the television industry, working in tandem with governmental agencies like the CRTC, has justified their economic interests we can see how television has come to be understood as a unique manifestation of the Canadian public sphere in need of protection. Furthermore, in deconstructing these arguments, an alternative path for television can be shown that critically re-evaluates the need for a single national rhetoric and opens up discussion for a more fluid and politically grounded sense of multiculturalism in lived practice.

THE PRODUCERS

In the midst of the 2004 federal election the Canadian actor Paul Gross spoke at a press conference announcing a campaign to bring culture to the forefront of political debate. It is somewhat fitting that Gross assumed this role since he is well known as both a stage and screen veteran – about as close to a celebrity as English Canada has. He was also the star of a failed Canadian television experiment in the mid-1990s when the short lived program *Due South*, about a Canadian mountie working in Chicago, was picked up by CBS. This was the first Canadian dramatic series to land on the primetime schedule of a Big 3 American network, where it ran for a very shaky two seasons. At the beginning of June 2004, Gross addressed a gathering of the Alliance of Canadian Cinema, Television and Radio Artists (ACTRA) in Toronto, telling them that Canada will never have a robust national culture on a purely volunteer basis and that candidates in the election campaign should be challenged as to where they stand ("Government must" 2004). Speaking specifically about the decision of Canadian mega-media company Alliance-Atlantis to withdraw from domestic cultural production, Gross argued that Alliance and Atlantis had become rich as a result of generous Canadian cultural policies, and that now they owed a debt to the Canadian people who had long subsidized them. While Gross was pleased with the CRTC's offer of increased advertising opportunities for broadcasters who air additional Canadian drama, he argued that the carrot needed to be accompanied by a stick in order to deal with "the unholy mess we have found ourselves in." ("Canadian TV" 2004). Later in the month, Gross and other ACTRA members hosted a news conference at CBC's Barbara Frum Atrium in Toronto to draw attention to cuts in government funding to Canadian film and television, the increasing amount of American television on Canadian airwaves, and the avoidance of cultural issues in the campaign for the June 28 election (Quill 2004). Despite these efforts, cultural issues never became an important part of the election itself. What Gross and his colleagues did accomplish was a reassertion of nationalist sympathies without any change in the business of television. In fact, according to a CRTC study released in March 2006, broadcasters spend approximately four times as much on imported programs as they do on indigenous productions, even while profits continue to climb higher every year (CRTC 2006).

For artists, actors, writers, directors, and other cultural producers involved in the creation of television, the government is an incredibly powerful force. Among the key issues for cultural producers are funding, access, and autonomy – each of which is variously guaranteed or threatened by the government on a regular basis. It is widely assumed by cultural producers, Gross among them, that without government subsidies for the cultural arena, Canada's television culture would simply evaporate. The assumption, created over the course of a half-century of experience, is that private broadcasters in Canada, despite their rapid proliferation in the digital age, will always opt for low-cost imported programming over original Canadian content unless they are required to air made-in-Canada material. This assumption seems accurate in light of broadcasters' expenditures, and it becomes more obvious at a glance at the primetime program listings on CTV, Global or CHUM-owned channels, which are replete with imported programming. For cultural producers, it is incumbent on the government to provide access by requiring private broadcasters to carry Canadian shows, and to finance the shows that they require those networks to deliver.

In an effort to bridge the divide between public and private broadcasting, or between artistic and industrial imperatives, the Canadian Television Fund was created in 1996. This is a joint enterprise between the Department of Canadian Heritage, Telefilm Canada, a crown corporation providing grants for film production, and the Cable Production Fund, operated by the cable industry. As it attests on its website, the goal of the CTF is to "encourage the financing and broadcasting of high-quality Canadian television productions" as well as to "reflect Canada to Canadians." While the CTF should be seen as an example of successful partnering between the public and private sector, it has been under the constant cloud of cutbacks since 2003, sometimes forcing the abrupt cancellation of Canadian shows that are otherwise perceived to be doing well. The leading private networks have become so reliant on the CTF that cuts to its budget are taken as an excuse to move away from their commitment to air Canadian content. In the words of CTV senior vice-president Bill Mustos, "We are facing a year where our federal funding is sharply reduced. In that context, we have to really be prudent about which shows we put forward for that funding" ("Canadian dramas axed" 2004). After a great deal of lobbying, and facing a general concern that Canadian television would surely die without a fully funded CTF, the Liberal government did not follow through on its threats to reduce the CTF budget to $62.5 million but instead returned it to its pre-cut level of $100 million. This change of heart came with stipulations, however, some of which did not sit well with some cultural producers. After using the nationalist argument to win back their funding, they seemed shocked that the Canadian government would tighten legislation around what counts as "Canadian stories."

In February 2005, *The Globe and Mail* reported that many Canadian documentary filmmakers were complaining that the CTF's focus on Canadian-themed programming made it "Orwellian." Comparing the subsidy system to political pressures that existed in the Soviet Union, Simcha Jacobovici argued that the lack of guaranteed funding for documentary filmmakers meant, "You're editing with the knowledge that they can pull the rug out from under you at any time. That's a terrible threat. It can bankrupt you" (Posner 2005). While Jacobovici's comparison of Canadian subsidies to filmmakers and television producers to the Soviet system may seem absurd, it highlights a difficult tension between culture as national heritage and culture as aesthetic production. It also raises questions about the very idea of a distinct national identity, even as artists themselves raise it to secure their own funding base. Less than a year after ACTRA intervened in the federal election to insist upon a strong, nationalist program that would create a distinct and identifiable Canadian culture, members of its association complained about the fact that the program was designed specifically to ensure Canadian distinctiveness.

Following ACTRA's logic, it seems that the position of television producers is that the government should finance Canada's television producers and also provide a broadcast platform in order to ensure the continuation of high-quality Canadian alternatives to international programming. At the same time, however, the government should stay out of the decision-making process and simply allow cultural producers the freedom to produce works that they, and their broadcast partners, deem best. The assumption that enriching private broadcasters and individual private production companies is what is best for the nation should, it follows, be borne out by the high degree of satisfaction that Canadian viewers have with Canadian programming. Yet, given the absence of that satisfaction, the conclusion among cultural producers is frequently to bemoan the poor viewing habits of Canadians while seeking out new funding opportunities. Cultural producers, the argument goes, serve the national good, even if the nation doesn't always realize it, and they should be funded and left to do their own thing.

The problem with this "have our cake and eat it too" approach isn't readily solved as long as Canadian television remains stuck in a nationalist sensibility that is rooted in protection from the monster to the south. However, the criticisms of the CTF's policy of monitoring funded productions for their inclusion of distinct Canadian content is an important one both in terms of the federal government's insistence on economic viability and in considering a more nuanced, political view of multiculturalism. Documentary filmmakers were especially vocal on this issue because of the restraints placed on the idea of what constitutes a matter of interest to Canadians. The other side of the argument is that they rightly criticized an outdated model of "hockey and doughnuts" in producing Canadian culture and challenged the essentialist argument about national identity in favour of a more compensatory model in which the definition of Canadianness in any cultural product isn't based on content as much as on quality, edification, and openness toward other cultures. It is that latter notion that helps to reawaken the multiculturalism debate and place it within new political and economic realities.

The demographics of Canada are changing to such a degree that it is only a matter of a few years before "visible minorities" will become the majority in cities like Toronto, Montreal, and Vancouver. Following from the principles of multiculturalism, how can such accelerated hybridity be reduced to a series of essentialist ideals for Canada that are based on Anglophone, northern, and Euro-western values? Second, as cultural producers are expected to prove their fiscal responsibility by selling their shows outside the Canadian market, the need for greater latitude in expressing alternative perspectives becomes more urgent. What is at stake for producers, then, is the degree to which the old models of Canadian protectionism are beginning to fail culturally, politically, and economically. Small-scale production companies cannot, and for the most part do not, try to compete directly in the American system. Instead, and echoing the economic policies of the former Liberal prime minister, Jean Chrétien, they feel they are better off seeking alliances with countries with similar political economies in which joint partnerships through co-productions, distribution deals, and the like expand the market for Canadian cultural goods. This process is about implicating Canadian cultural production within a global mediascape of shared cultural sectors, frameworks, networks, and finance schemes in order to create a greater sense of multiplicity and diversity on the airwaves. It is not clear that the artists who complained see this potential themselves, and certainly the position of ACTRA during the 2004 election suggests that they are still clinging tightly to the federal lifeline of essentialist Canadian culture. However, in taking their criticisms seriously and not just as the petulant whining of a pampered elite, there is the possibility of discovering promising new directions for re-thinking what Canadian culture can accomplish.

THE BROADCASTERS

Canada's national broadcasters make similar claims as cultural producers about their own centrality to the project of building a nation-state, but clearly their arguments are more economically than artistically oriented. As such, they seem to always be working to expand their scope beyond the borders that they themselves have erected. Even more than artists, therefore, the broadcasting sector has tied its success and failures to a near exclusive relationship to the United States, both as a market of unlimited and cheap product and as an imminent competitor. As an advertising-based medium, television depends on gaining the largest possible share of audience to sell back to potential advertisers. However, as the broadcast spectrum expands and reorganizes itself into niche markets based on specialty or subscription-based channels, the audience fragments and can no longer be as neatly packaged in large, homogenous groups. This is not to suggest that television viewing is necessarily declining to dangerously low levels, dragging profits down with them as some broadcasters may argue as they clamber to reduce restrictions on Canadian content requirements. Rather, revenue is increasing but it's increasingly spread between individual stations, and viewership for specific programs is less stable.

While the changing economics of broadcasting from homogenous, mass media to a more fractured, disjunctured media could potentially open up new levels of opportunity and risk-taking, the attitude of broadcasters has been to shore up a defence against change rather than embrace new logics. This reliance on a survivor-victim mentality that is dependent almost exclusively on a perceived rivalry with the United States has led to strategies intended to secure market advantage at the lowest possible costs. The most important of these, adopted almost wholesale by the private broadcasters CTV and Global, is the process of purchasing Canadian broadcast rights for popular American network shows and then showing them in simultaneous substitution. That means that Canadian broadcasters grab the signal from the networks at the same time as it airs in the United States but insert their own advertising and station identifiers. This dependency model is predicated on a rather self-serving claim to preserve Canadian values by ensuring that the invisible ownership structure behind the airing of any show remains Canadian. By that we mean that Canadian networks exploit American commercialism and Canadian nationalism simultaneously by insisting that American broadcasters cannot invade our sovereign territory but can only borrow the airwaves. Meanwhile, Canadian broadcasters benefit from reduced start-up costs and risks associated with creating new programming while inserting their own advertisers' commercials to secure revenue. It highlights the way that culture and economics, content and form, have been neatly separated out from each other. Further, it gives some insight into how both economic arguments of free markets and cultural arguments for nationalist protectionism can share common ground within a liberal framework of choice.

This tactic has certainly not escaped the notice of cultural nationalists who eventually won a campaign to keep the CBC, the public broadcaster, from relying on this rather backhanded form of distinct Canadian broadcasting. Furthermore, the trade-off for simultaneous substitution is that Canadian content regulations require private broadcasters to offer some measure of indigenous programming during an overly generous definition of primetime hours. As a result, broadcasters have also looked for ways to again circumvent the risk involved in producing new programming while still conforming to protectionist policies that they themselves have benefited from. Rather than turn to dramatic or narrative series, which are probably the most costly and high-risk form of television, the trend has been for Canadian companies to feature news and informational programming to make up the bulk of their required Canadian content.

Another strategy of broadcasters to preserve a nationalist monopoly on the airwaves is to mimic whole channels in a revamped Canadian context. The CHUM-City group has been especially successful in preventing such American stalwarts as MTV and VH1 from being available in Canada and offering up their own stations MuchMusic, MusiquePlus and MuchMoreMusic instead. Now, as MTV Canada has finally entered into the market by recasting itself as a talk and lifestyle channel, rather than a music one, the Canadian channels are scrambling to fill huge holes in their programming schedule that were once filled with imported fare like *MTV Cribs*, *Pimp My Ride*, and others. Canada's special digital channel MenTV has lost a number of battles to have the American-based Spike TV, which went from a country and western channel to a men's programming channel in 2004, taken off basic extended cable service. Perhaps the most protected specialty niche channel in the Canadian system is CBC's Newsworld, the twenty-four-hour news channel that is required to be carried on basic cable. While other channels, including the American giant CNN, are available to cable and satellite subscribers, only Newsworld is guaranteed for all cable subscribers. It is not the most popular information station – that credit goes to the Weather Network – but it does serve a very important symbolic function by ensuring that Canadians can enjoy a full evening of American dramatic programming while their information on world events will come directly from nationally protected sources. About the only original Canadian station that did not have an obvious and already successful American counterpart when it was launched was PrideTV, a station devoted to gay and lesbian issues that was subject to harsh restrictions by skittish cable systems, turned to scheduling pornography in an effort to boost audiences, and, in March 2005, splintered into two channels: the lifestyle-oriented OutTV and the adult entertainment channel, HARD on Pridevision.

Thus, with few exceptions, it appears that the business model adopted by Canadian broadcasters can only be defined through their apparent need to play it safe, avoid risk, and minimize costs. Leave programming decisions to the American networks and produce only low-cost, low-risk local programming for the Canadian market, while launching specialty channels that are carbon copies of successful American channels. What differentiates the Canadian system from the American system is the way that "culture" is deployed effectively to offset both criticisms of the profiteering model of private broadcasting as well as the threats of opening the sector to foreign competition. Canadian broadcasters largely rely on the ominous presence of American television from which it borrows with one hand while denouncing it as an enemy with the other. Efforts to move beyond this very narrow binary are limited by protectionist policies that prevent foreign ownership even though Canadian media conglomerates are investing heavily in joint ventures around the globe. For example, France recently altered its policies so that even English-language co-productions with Canada can be considered "European" for the purposes of subsidies (Collins 2002, 133). Thus, the Canadian industry benefits from a relaxation of regulations in other countries that they themselves balk at domestically.

In an ideal world for Canadian broadcasters, a one-way road to globalization in which Canadian culture could flow out in the form of products and ownership while foreign products would be stopped at the border would be the ideal situation, and in many ways that model is already in place. The justification for this practice is, as always, the perceived threat from the United States. Yet, despite the clamourings to protect Canadian airwaves from American incursion, the industry relies heavily on American product. So in the name of Canadian national identity, the Canadian MTV is a talk channel rather than a music channel and MuchMusic enjoys a competition-free existence in the market for music videos, even with the loss of many of its popular imported programs. A similar situation has existed for MuchMusic's sister station MuchMoreMusic and its relationship with VH1. The nationalist argument from broadcasters is that this arrangement means that Canadians are not robbed of popular American programming but they see it on a channel that also promotes an indigenous Canadian music industry, which is held to be a net benefit to the nation. Choice and patriotism are served in equal measure. While on the surface that line of reasoning appears to make sense, at its core is a fundamental assumption that Canadians will not watch Canadian programming unless forced to. Thus, broadcasters first invoke the rhetoric of choice to have these programs available and then claim a nationalist argument of protection to limit any consumer choice that could potentially negatively affect them.

What is interesting is the extent to which the CRTC has agreed with broadcasters and established a regulatory framework in which Canadian viewers are offered primarily channels that the industry itself regards as uncompetitive and second-rate, such as the rather hapless SpikeTV. Canadian viewers are restricted in their choice, the argument goes, for the good of the nation, so that broadcasters can operate in a relatively competition-free market which, they argue, benefits Canadian viewers even when they themselves might not choose the options or care to support them. What is interesting is that, though they regularly invoke anti-American rhetoric to justify Canadian protectionist policy, the result is a highly Americanized broadcasting system, rather than a more globalized system that would be in keeping with Canadian notions of multiculturalism. It raises significant questions about Canadian culture and its homogenizing tendencies from within, which resist innovative, culturally diverse programming and model themselves after American networks in ways that preserve a dominant sense of anglocentric, white Canadianness.

THE CABLE INDUSTRY

For many cultural producers, the enemy that looms largest on the horizon is the cable industry. While television producers like ACTRA cannot complain too aggressively about the government that pays their bills or the broadcasters that provide their platform, the cable industry, which exists at a remove from these cultural concerns, is the player whose profit-driven motives are most naked in the field of Canadian television. Like the Conservative party, the cable industry claims to champion the rights of individual Canadian viewers through the provision of choice. This is a useful and popular rhetoric, although the consequences of unlimited consumer choice are always carefully concealed, and, in fact, genuine choice is never really presented as an option. Unlike television producers, who often wrap themselves in the Canadian flag when presenting their case, the cable industry is more loath to frame their interests as anything other than profit maximization and conceptualizes the audience less as citizens than as consumers. The primary, some would say exclusive, goal of the cable industry is the expansion of shareholder profits. Profits are generated by creating demand, finding new customers, offering new services, and reducing costs. This places the cable industry in the clearest alignment with Canadian viewers because in order to sell services to Canadians they must have offerings that we will find attractive. Yet, their business practices often work harder to curtail viewer expectations than to facilitate their needs.

If the cable industry recognizes that the road forward to profitability relies primarily on their ability to find new and improved services to offer consumers (such as internet-based phone services), it also recognizes that the CRTC and its defence of the existing regulatory framework often act as a roadblock. It is clear, for example, that if the CRTC licensed ESPN or HBO for broadcast in Canada, many television viewers would leap at the opportunity to subscribe. This has allowed the cable industry to position itself as the voice of Canadian consumer choice in its discursive war with the CRTC and private broadcasters. Nonetheless, the industry has actively opposed genuine viewer choice in the form of à la carte cable offerings. The possibility of allowing viewers to pay for only those channels that they wish to watch, rather than purchasing channels in mandatory bundles, is feared for the possibility that it could erode cable industry profits. Studies in the United States by Nielsen Media Research indicate that the average television viewer watches only seventeen channels regularly (Lazarus 2004) but subscribers to the most inclusive cable and satellite packages pay for hundreds of channels, most of which remain unwatched. For the cable industry, à la carte selections would likely entail a reduction of services purchased by consumers, and, consequently, a decline in profitability. At the same time, the logic of supply and demand indicates that individual channels would have to reduce their cost to consumers in order to compete for viewers, and, consequently, advertisers, further eroding the profitability of the cable industry. In February 2006, the CRTC ruled that television consumers should have the ability to purchase channels in an à la carte system but opted to maintain the current system until at least 2010 (Robertson and McLean 2006a,b). Despite the cable industry's rhetoric about supporting consumer choice, it is clear that this is a mask for expanding the profitability of an industry that, at its heart, rejects the very thing that it claims to be championing.

The fact that five companies own almost 90 per cent of the cable market is only one of the most striking features about the organization of this industry (Beaty and Sullivan 2003, 152). Even more problematic is the fact that they have effectively carved up the country into different territories in order to prevent any real competition amongst each other. Rogers is by far the largest cable company and encompasses most of central Canada. They were able to acquire so much of the market in part through a swap with Shaw Cable that allows that company to dominate the west. Cogeco takes up what part of Ontario Rogers doesn't control, while Vidéotron dominates Quebec. Finally, Eastlink, the smallest of the big five, owns most of the Maritime market. For consumers, this arrangement means there is no actual choice of cable providers, except for the small satellite service market. With a near-captive market, individual cable companies create their own carefully limited form of choice by bundling various channels and services and developing a series of packages instead of allowing viewers to pick-and-choose their own selection. Complaints about this business practice, especially the rather suspect anti-competition agreement between cable companies, are generally justified as necessary to ensure a strong, independent, national industry. In other words, the very companies who argue in favour of a consumerist model of choice are just as quick as their counterparts to lay claim to a notion of sovereign nationalism if it means protective and preferential regulatory systems. However, as technologies dismantle territories, it is becoming harder for the cable industry in Canada to prevent foreign competition from ruining what is, for them, a near-perfect system.

The clearest rival to the Canadian cable industry comes not from within but from foreign broadcasting systems that better meet the needs of increasingly more powerful multicultural communities that are not as easily seduced by the homogenic rhetoric of Canadian national identity. There have been some small measures to respond to these audience desires. For example, recent debates about the addition of so-called third-language television channels (non-French and non-English channels, often from overseas) have been supported by the cable industry in order to attract a multilingual Canadian viewership, especially in dense urban areas, but the coverage of these channels is scattered across the country. While efforts to expand linguistic and cultural options are proceeding at a snail's pace, the cable industry has dedicated far more energy to import well-branded American channels, including Fox News, HBO, ESPN, and Nickelodeon, to Canadian airwaves, a strategy that preserves a sense of a homogeneous mass Canadian audience that is just like that in the United States. Their chief argument for this business strategy is, they say, to counteract the damaging effects of viewers going outside the country to purchase television services from foreign satellite operators. Broadcasters have used simultaneous substitution to avoid the competition of American-based networks. The cable industry responds by simply reversing their free market stance and lobbying to keep foreign-owned provider systems out of Canada while allowing their own companies to offer the same services in the name of national unity.

THE VIEWERS

At times the financial interests of television producers, networks, and cable companies radically diverge and battles are waged for regulators to decide, while at other moments the entire industry comes together in a common cause. One such cause revolves around the issue of so-called "satellite signal theft," which pits viewers against industry in ways that challenge both economic and cultural arguments for protectionism. The issue of satellite signal theft has been a front-burner issue for several years now, particularly since the formation of the Coalition Against Satellite Signal Theft (CASST) to lobby government for stiffer penalties and to try to convince Canadians that signal theft is not a victimless crime. The Canadian Cable Television Association (CCTA) claims that approximately 700,000 illegal satellite dishes were operating in Canada in September 2002 (Yale 2002). Their definition of "illegal" does not mean stolen, however, but also includes Canadians who purchase satellite service from anyone other than a regulated Canadian-owned company. Thus, it has been dubbed a grey market economy. This distinction between grey and black markets was apparently lost on the Supreme Court of Canada when it ruled one year previously that the decoding of encrypted signals originating from a foreign distributor, even if you paid for the privilege, contravened the Radiocommunication Act. However, a Quebec court ruled in October 2004 that the ban on grey market satellite systems was unconstitutional on the grounds that it was a violation of the Charter of Rights and Freedoms. The ultimate dispensation of that case is still pending. Regardless, it is clear from the Radiocommunication Act that there is a belief among successive Canadian governments that television broadcasting is a unique medium deserving of cultural protections unheard of in other cases. No laws forbid the purchase by Canadians of foreign newspapers, magazines, books, compact discs, or DVDs. Further, no laws require Canadians to purchase these forms of media from Canadian companies, from Chapters.ca, for example, instead of Amazon.com. But television is tightly controlled so that the government may ensure that Canadians access only authorized national outlets.

While the argument against American broadcasters is based on the belief that it will lead to a homogenous, hegemonic industry controlling television and curtailing the proliferation of multicultural voices that distinguishes Canada, the reality seems to be the opposite. As Appadurai points out, this is not surprising. The invocation of a major external threat is a common tactic to secure the controlling interest of the hegemonic forces within (1990, 296). According to the CCTA, one of the prime motivators for grey market satellite use is consumer choice and cultural diversity – precisely the issue that the CCTA claims to be most interested in as an organization. In the simplest terms, American satellite providers offer a wider selection of channels than do Canadian providers. This discrepancy is particularly pronounced in the case of ethnic language television channels. For example, on regular analog signals, Canadian television offers only four alternative language services: Telelatino (TLN) for Italian and Spanish, Fairchild TV which broadcasts in Mandarin and Cantonese, SATV for South Asian audiences, and Odyssey, which serves the Greek community. In addition to this, there is limited penetration of the forty-four licensed Category 2 ethnic digital specialty services. Category 2 channels mean that the CRTC has approved them for broadcast but do not require any cable company to actually make them available for subscribers. For instance, while Rogers Cable in the Toronto area made available to its subscribers channels in Portuguese, Punjabi, Korean, and Urdu, ethnic television choices were severely restricted in other parts of the country, and nowhere is the full slate of forty-four channels available.

The significance of the grey market satellite industry to ongoing debates about television's role in reproducing national cultural identity is that it shifts the discussion away from the usual concerns about American incursion by bringing the issue of ethnic language channel selection to the forefront. For example, while in 2003, there was only half a channel broadcast in Spanish in Canada (with four and a half additional Spanish-language channels authorized to broadcast but not necessarily picked up by cable companies in 2004), the American satellite leader DirecTV offered a total of thirty-one such channels. For Canadians wanting television in Spanish, the choice was seemingly clear-cut. This and other instances of multilinguistic and cultural communities not being properly served by Canadian television is a significant factor in the rise of grey market satellite. Canadian broadcasters and regulatory agencies want to present this issue as a necessary form of cultural protection from the American television behemoth. Yet, with the wide access to U.S. cable programming on Canadian channels, the idea that grey market is being used predominantly to get HBO does not hold up. This claim does, however, serve both corporate and governmental agendas to continue protectionist policies that have less to do with keeping American influence out than with securing a particular, homogenic brand of Canadian nationalism.

In this sense, then, the idea of Canada as a nation can be more readily seen as not much more than a discursive trope bolstering the legitimacy of state and capital interests. The relationship between nation/state/culture is at the crux of the organization of television. It is important, therefore, to reiterate that our focus remains exclusively on the English Canadian experience because it is there that the state is fully formed while national ideals remains problematic, with the potential to undermine the stability of the state. If, as Erin Manning argues, the rise of the sovereign state is the hallmark of modernity (2003, xix), while national identity is its fundamental form of subjectivity (Mackey 1999, 4), then culture can be understood as a mediating force that is used by each to legitimate the other. What this means is that television is controlled by the state in order to promote a unified sense of national identity that will in turn justify the state's continued authority. Similarly, and concurrently, cultural nationalists turn to the state to protect television from destabilizing forces using the claim of American hegemony. However, and perhaps more urgently, the less clear-cut, more diffuse enemy from within lurks in the shadows of this argument: those Canadian citizens who fail or even outright refuse to conform to an equally hegemonic notion of unified national identity where multicultural tolerance only goes so far. In other words, Canadian viewers who desire more than half a channel of television in Spanish are criminalized for failing to maintain their status as marginalized multicultural others.

In response to industry complaints about the loss of customers to unauthorized foreign satellite providers, the government took a tough albeit hollow stance on satellite signal theft with new legislation that shows how easily the fear of the "other" is namelessly invoked. Introduced in February 2004, Bill C-2 would have amended the Radiocommunication Act to significantly increase the penalties for retransmitting or decoding an unauthorized signal. This bill, which died on the table and has not been revived, angered a large number of ethnic groups across the country, as it was seen as a direct attack on cultural diversity and an attempt to criminalize the cultural choices of a large number of Canadians whose interests are not being served by the existing regulatory framework. In July 2004, the CRTC attempted to assuage these concerns by authorizing nine new non-Canadian third-language services. These new channels, whose authorization was ostensibly intended to help fight signal theft (CRTC 2004a), included general interest channels in German and Romanian, four Spanish channels, a Spanish and Portuguese movie service, and two Arabic channels. While this move was intended to open the airwaves to more international competition from foreign-based media companies, three decisions by the CRTC suggest that far more scrutiny should be placed on the regulatory process. In 2004, two foreign-language channels were denied licences on the grounds of Canadian cultural protection. One channel, however, received permission to broadcast on the basis of an argument that it would alleviate grey market satellite purchases. That the two denied were foreign language, and the one successful application was the wealthy American channel Fox News Network calls into question how much the CRTC really believes its own rhetoric of fostering Canadian identity in a multicultural environment against an American homogenous tyrant.

THE CRTC: SERVANT TO WHICH MASTER?

When the CRTC announced the licensing of new foreign-language channels, it sought to downplay those channels whose applications were denied. Four Spanish, one Arabic, and one Italian channel lost their bids for authorization. Of these, the one that raised the most eyebrows was RAI International, the extremely popular broadcaster from Italy. Canada has one of the highest per capita populations of Italian immigrants in the world and yet it barely serves this community with one-half of a channel, Telelatino or TLN, which is owned by Corus Entertainment. The hearings at the CRTC pitted the economic interests of the cable industry (CCTA) who would benefit from increased channel subscriptions by including RAI, against those of the Canadian broadcasters (represented by the Canadian Association of Broadcasters, or CAB), whose members feared increased competition for viewers, and escalating prices for foreign programming. Ultimately, the CRTC rejected any foreign-language channels that were perceived to threaten the economic interests of established or proposed Canadian-owned channels, despite demands from within ethnic communities for greater viewing options. RAI certainly fit this description since it had a programming contract with TLN that it had cancelled in anticipation of launching its own signal, and indicated that it would not consider partnering with Canadian companies. What is most problematic in the reasoning of the CRTC is the fact that it included channels that only existed on paper in its assessment of how linguistic communities were being served, even if they had never broadcasted so much as a minute. Thus, Corus Entertainment argued that licensing RAI International, an Italian-based company, harmed its own ability to launch RAI Canada – which it had not done, and which it had no immediate plans to do. The argument may have worked in Ottawa, but it failed to sway a community frustrated over the lack of television about its home culture and language. A petition signed by more than 100,000 Italian Canadians requested access to the popular channel, and Italian-Canadian politicians publicly voiced their support, lobbying the CRTC to review its decision.

In the face of widespread anger, the CRTC amended the regulations regarding third-language general interest television channels, allowing them to be available to viewers who also subscribed to the Canadian channel against which they most directly compete. Thus, Canadians can now legally subscribe to RAI International as long as they also subscribe to Telelatino, assuming that the cable companies offer both services. Unfortunately, this new-found openness did not extend to foreign niche channels, which remain barred in Canada if they compete with a similar Canadian niche channel. Therefore, for example, it is possible for an Italian movie channel to receive a licence but only if no similar Canadian-owned channel has already been licensed. This decision strikes at the heart of Canada's claims to multiculturalism and tells us something about our own hegemonic control of the airwaves. Existing Canadian specialty channels featuring arts and culture rely almost exclusively on English-language programming. Similarly, sports television devotes only a small amount of time to international competitions, and often dub in English commentary for English-speaking audiences. Dozens of English-language general interest and niche channels are authorized for carriage in Canada, but the CRTC continues to maintain roadblocks to more comprehensive offerings for linguistic minorities, maintaining these groups in the television age of the 1960s with one or two channels, while the dominant linguistic group is provided hundreds of channels. The CRTC's policies minimize foreign-language intervention into Canadian airwaves, keeping linguistic minorities in secure cubbyholes that ensure Anglophone cultural dominance. Foreign culture is restricted to the marginalized space of multiculturalism, where values of folk, tradition, and heritage prevent them from influencing the aesthetic authority of English Canada.

In July 2004 no issue put the problems of the Canadian broadcasting system in perspective as much as the licensing of the Qatar-based Arabic-language news channel, Aljazeera. The authorization of Aljazeera was supported by Canada's Arab and Muslim population, but opposed by many members of the Jewish population on the grounds that its programming was anti-Semitic. More than 1,200 comments were filed in support of Aljazeera, and more than 500 were filed in opposition with the CRTC. The significant issue revolved around accusations made by the Canadian Jewish Congress and others that "under the guise of a seemingly legitimate news agency, Aljazeera has provided hatemongers and terrorists with a platform for their views" (CRTC 2004b). The CRTC rejected this characterization of the channel for lack of proof but did rule that there was credible evidence that Aljazeera *could* include abusive commentary that might be contrary to Canadian law in the future. Based on this guilty-until-proven-innocent ruling, and because the CRTC's licensing power does not extend to non-Canadian networks or channels, it ruled that cable and satellite companies distributing Aljazeera would be held responsible for its content. In a general climate of post-9/11 anti-Arab hysteria, such a ruling had a decidedly chilling effect. Michael Hennessy, president of the CCTA, indicated that this form of prior restraint "sets a frightening precedent and virtually ensures that no distributor will ever carry this service in Canada" (Mah 2004). The requirements that distributors delete anti-Semitic or other offensive programming meant, according to Shaw Communications president Peter Bissonnette, that each cable or satellite company would have to hire a twenty-four-hour monitor of the channel, fluent in Arabic and conversant in contemporary broadcasting standards (Mah 2004). The decision, therefore, paid lip service to traditional Canadian notions of openness and tolerance, while, in practice, it kept a critical, alternative news voice off the air. It is interesting that the same provision was not made for the licensing of Fox News Network in November 2004, despite the fact that the network has frequently been cited for its bigoted intolerance of racial, gender, and linguistic minorities and has often taken an explicit anti-Canadian stance in its commentaries.

The example of Fox provides the final piece in the puzzle of how the CRTC comes to make decisions that privilege American-based companies over other international broadcasters, while continuing to use the spectre of Americanized airwaves to further cultural protectionist measures that only seem to keep foreign language and multicultural programming off the air. On November 18, 2004, the CRTC ruled that Fox News was eligible to be added to the list of digital channels offered to Canadians by cable and satellite companies. The request to add the channel had come from the CCTA, who argued that bringing Fox News to Canada would expand the channel choice offered to Canadians, increase the appeal of the digital cable tier as a whole, and help combat grey market satellite services. The request was opposed by CAB, who argued that licensing the channel would reward Fox News for withdrawing from a joint Canadian proposal (the CRTC had licensed Fox News Canada in December 2000 as a channel to be owned and operated by Fox News and Global, but the channel was never launched), and by a number of individuals who criticized the station's conservative political bias. The request was supported by conservative Canadian political groups, such as REAL Women and B'Nai Brith, on the grounds that the conservative political bias would be a welcome addition to the Canadian political media landscape. Even though the CRTC had precedent not only in the way it ruled against Aljazeera, but also in its denial to RAI International, who similarly withdrew from a joint partnership with Corus to produce RAI Canada, it steered clear of the politics this time. The debate rested solely on the economics of whether the channel would compete with established Canadian news channels, Newsworld and CTV Newsnet. While the CRTC had rejected the addition of Fox News in November 2003, a year later it ruled that Fox does not compete with those channels because it is largely editorially based rather than news based, and further that there was no conflict because "Fox News offers little or no Canadian coverage" (CRTC 2004b).

The CRTC's reversal of its 2003 position, coming in the wake of months of sustained criticism of the regulatory agency and on the heels of the Aljazeera and RAI decisions, appears bizarre. First, the regulator welcomed Fox News to Canada largely because it was a channel that pays no attention to Canadian news, a somewhat dubious criterion for allowing a channel into the country, and particularly troubling given that it could not be argued to provide an international perspective by any stretch of the imagination. Second, many opponents of Fox News had suggested that the news organization should be held to the same standards that the CRTC had imposed on Aljazeera, particularly given their history of supporting American isolationism and hateful commentaries on any group, community, or nation that they perceive to contest that supremacy. The CRTC rejected this suggestion, citing a lack of sufficient cause for believing that Fox broadcasts hateful comments. Less than two weeks after announcing their ruling, however, conservative columnist Ann Coulter appeared on Fox News' *Hannity and Colmes* program arguing that Canada had become an enemy of the United States, that Canadians are a legitimate target of hate because they speak French, and that "they are lucky we allow them to exist on the same continent" ("Canada is lucky" 2004). Thus, 'in many ways, Fox News represents everything that the CRTC is supposed to ward against: American hegemonic incursion; racial, ethnic, and cultural intolerance; and the undermining of a distinct Canadian identity. However, it is worth stressing at this point that our argument isn't that Fox News should not have been allowed into Canada. Rather, we want to point out that its licensing against the backdrop of the rulings against RAI and Aljazeera exposes the hypocrisy of Canadian broadcasting policy that claims to be serving a nation but really seems to be only serving a state.

Given the fact that the CRTC explicitly licensed Fox News because of, rather than despite, its near total lack of Canadian content, it would appear likely that the primary motivation for the decision resides in an ongoing policy framework that cannot see beyond the Canada-U.S. border. The winning arguments in the end were economic ones against the imagined bogeyman of grey market satellite completely dismantling the Canadian broadcasting industry. Yet, those same arguments failed to sway regulators in favour of foreign language services that could effectively counter the crushing wave of homogenous programming that is claimed as the end result of allowing American television to spill over the border. In the end, Fox News was added in the hopes that the growth of the grey market might be slowed and the expansion of digital cable penetration would be enhanced through access to carefully selected networks. However, it cannot be overlooked that the first station to gain this new access was a powerful, vocal, and wealthy American station that is well known for ethnic, cultural, and linguistic intolerance. It appears that Canada continues to believe its own protectionist argument about American hegemony, only now it is aiding and abetting that hegemony. Foreign content that does not fall within the rubric of white, western values is much easier for regulators to keep out of the country. But if the CRTC truly wants to expand the airwaves to non-Canadian perspectives, why license another English-language North American-based service? What really is the logic behind letting Fox in but keeping Aljazeera out? How might television alter the perspective of Canadians if the CRTC took its commitment to multiculturalism seriously? Two distinct but related alternatives shed light on these questions. First, the fact that European television policy has adopted an increasingly Canadian approach in its own dealings with the public/private split. Second, Canadian community television, as the third pillar in the broadcasting sector, helps to expose a decidedly liberal bias in the promotion of television as the electronic public sphere.

ALTERNATIVE AIRWAVES: COMMUNITY TELEVISION AND EUROPEAN BROADCASTING IN CONTEXT

In the Lincoln report, community television was praised as an important aspect of national cultural identity. The CRTC has been working with stakeholders to create more "access programming," as it is called, but they are caught in a bind between two conceptions of what is most important: programming *for* communities or programming *by* communities. This conundrum also raises the thorny issue of what is meant by community. Cable companies insist that community must be limited to geographic fixity; therefore, access programming must be done by those living within a certain radius and only seen by people in that same area. Otherwise, community television might encroach on commercial ventures in multilinguistic or ethnic channels. The result is that if the Italian community in Montreal wants to create a program that could be seen and enjoyed by their counterparts in Toronto, Vancouver, or Halifax, it does not qualify as "community television." One result is that community is defined very narrowly and subject to issues of physical proximity rather than cultural affinity. Marginalized groups remain isolated from each other, reinforcing their minority status as secondary cultures.

The example of community television can sometimes be overstated, given how few people actually watch it. Yet advocates argue that its value is not in conventional broadcasting criteria of production, programming, and audience. Rather, its contribution can be found in the process of the coming together of individuals to make television (Higgins 1999, 626). The origins of community television in North America stem from the National Film Board of Canada's "Challenge for Change" program in which everyday citizens were given camera equipment and encouraged to make their own films. Despite the lack of audience for these projects, it sparked an idea that video had, if not revolutionary potential, at least civic potential in terms of expanding media literacy and opening up the airwaves to ad-hoc, grassroots programming from the people (Higgins 1999, 631). In this sense, community television could fulfill the promise of the medium as a full-fledged electronic public sphere where individual voices could proliferate and thrive (King and Mele 1999, 621). As the Canadian Media Education Society in Canada argues, "the community channel is the first place we find participation and public access." Raising the spectre of Americanization, they argue on behalf of a generation who needs community television in order to develop a greater sense of civic belonging so that "new people with new ideas can find easy access." Yet they balk at the idea of these stations creating alliances with universities and other educational institutions, hoping to exclude volunteers who are on a professional career path (CMES 2001). The fetishization of amateurism poses a significant problem for the value of community television in Canada insofar as it curtails participatory action across geographic regions. A nostalgic longing for the physically localized community can just as easily breed isolationism as openness and can prevent communities from forming out of linguistic, ethnic, or other affinity subject positions, seriously curtailing television's potential to transcend physical borders. In this sense, Canada's vision of community television remains grounded in liberal notions of the public sphere where the virtue of individualism is extolled while the power of real community is kept in check through regulatory systems designed to put a homogeneous definition of national culture first.

It would be nice to look elsewhere in the world and see how other countries deal with the public/private/community divide more effectively. Yet, if anything, it seems as if the Canadian model is becoming the international standard. This is certainly the case in European countries, which are coming together in an effort to create a unified European market and a related culture. In the 1980s, the EU adopted Television Without Frontiers, a blueprint to break down national barriers to the airwaves. The goal was to find a better balance between local, regional, national, and transnational relationships, opening the market for more co-ventures, and investing the future of television in notions of consumer choice and market success (Iosifidis et al 2005, Collins 2002). The liberalization of broadcasting altered a largely public system by turning it into a hybrid of public and private, and forcing public broadcasters into more commercial models of audience share, fiscal prosperity, and international competition. The result is dismally familiar to Canadians. Hopes were pinned on the promise for new digital technologies to draw in bigger audiences, but these failed to appear. In fact, less than half of the EU's 140 million households had access to either cable or satellite television by 2000 (Iosifidis 2005, 63). Meanwhile, indigenous production declined as broadcasters began importing shows and whole channels from elsewhere, most notably the United States. Channels like CNN International, MTV Europe, and others filled the gaps created by this expansionary plan. The audiovisual deficit with the United States has climbed precipitously. The more that Europe liberalizes its markets under the umbrella of consumer choice, the more that both public television and private broadcasting are placed in crisis. The example of European "progress," coupled with community television's nostalgic sense of itself, demonstrates the need to retain some sense of nationalist discourse in television policy, albeit one that pays greater attention to communities of affinity, rather than geography. Without some measure of cultural protection and a regulatory system that ensures access for marginalized citizens, the worst-case scenario of globalization does really seem to come true.

CONCLUSION

While the television situation for some linguistic minorities in Canada has been showing signs of improvement, the partial measures taken by the CRTC cannot reasonably be seen as a significant effort to embrace a version of multiculturalism that moves beyond the liberal equivalence of it with depoliticized notions of heritage in a supporting role to one authentic national identity. The continued insistence on a narrow definition of community based on physical proximity furthers the erosion of any multiculturalism that might offer minorities a substantial public voice and concomitant political power. Thus, it appears that the CRTC still hopes to keep a tight lid on broadcasting while maintaining a façade of Canadian culture as open, accessible, and tolerant – up to a point. It is the job of the CRTC, apparently, to find a balance between, but keep as distinct categories, Canadian culture and multiculturalism, which it does primarily through supporting private industry with protectionist policies. However, given how difficult it has been to balance economics and culture, and the fact that regulators insist on seeing Canada in a very narrow continental context rather than a truly international one, it seems increasingly likely that in the future the CRTC will collapse under the weight of its own contradictions. The present system, with its emphasis on territorialism, sovereignty, and distinct national identity, will not stand up to the challenges faced by globalization. As long as it remains framed around negative connotations of commercialization, commodification, homogenization, and Americanization, Canadian broadcasting will maintain a defensive posture against globalization. Yet multiculturalism points to a different model in which the mediascape services new ideas, peoples, money, and technology as part of the flow of globalization. In fact, it may be better served by suggesting that these things do not flow as much as they flux. By that we mean that steady, controllable, and predictable airwaves – not to mention nation-states – will give way to increasingly more ad-hoc cross-currents of cultures, technologies, and ideologies. Furthermore, it means that the assumption that a distinct national culture is necessary for ensuring a sense of political allegiance is equally outmoded (Collins 1990, 8). Canada, with its longstanding emphasis on mass media systems as a tool of nation-building, has always held an ambivalent tension between nation and state, polity and culture, since these systems really serve a far more expansive vision than could be contained by territorialism. That is what makes television far from an outmoded or residual medium forged out of the modernist aims of cohesion, and ripe for the possibilities laid out by postmodern realities of disjuncture and difference, a triangulation between global, local, and national, and a re-imagining of cultural politics in which unity and sovereignty are not the goals. Thus, in considering television as perhaps the most highly regulated, most anxiously debated medium that has ever been put in the service of state authority and national identity, some exciting new directions come to light.

The fear of American co-optation of television is not completely unfounded, however, and would likely be realized through the adoption of the Conservative party platform. Rather than considering it from a position of Canadian national unity, however, the real concern stems from the risk to those small pockets of difference that currently exist on the dial. Supporters of the Tory deregulation plan argue that it would provide greatly enhanced consumer choice and channel availability, with cable and satellite companies acting quickly to bring popular American channels into Canada. This would likely be the case. Foreign language broadcasters may or may not follow, given the smaller and more diverse market share they would encounter. As the example of Europe has shown, rather than leading to a multi-lingual television landscape, Television Without Frontiers has hastened the rise of English-language programming across national spectra (Collins 2002, 35). In the current climate of market consolidation and the quest for expanding audience share, an economic logic of niche programming and small market ventures seems less viable even as they are the true heirs to an ideology of individualism, choice, and access. Instead, homogenization appears to continue to dominate. Third-language stations tend to be restricted to major urban centres like Toronto, Montreal, and Vancouver, or made available by foreign-owned satellite companies which do not have sufficient Canadian-based programming to satisfy regulatory agencies or reflect the specific localities of diasporic audiences. As the Conservatives seriously contemplate loosening foreign-ownership regulations, the possibility that American media companies like ComCast and DirecTV would acquire Canadian companies becomes more likely. Ultimately, if trends continue, it is possible that Canada would be brought completely under the influence of the broadcast industry of the United States and there would be little, or perhaps nothing, to differentiate our television culture from that of our southern neighbour.

Which Canadian channels would survive deregulation? Likely, very few. Take, for example, a network like APTN, which services Canada's aboriginal community by broadcasting in multiple languages and producing an enormous amount of original programming for northern populations. The channel, which draws most of its audience from one of Canada's most diverse and geographically scattered populations, is carried nation-wide because it is required by the CRTC. This allows the station to continue to exist and serve its constituents. Without mandatory carriage requirements, it is likely that most cable companies would discontinue the station, or move it to a subscriber-only basis, which would spell certain doom. The station would likely be replaced on the dial by an American network, removing a vital source of cultural communication for a historically marginalized community. Other channels would surely share similar fates. Established niche channels with loyal audiences – TSN, YTV, and MuchMusic – might be able to offset the flood of similar American channels, although they would suffer from the fact that so much of their programming is carried by ESPN, Nickelodeon, or MTV.

Canada's major networks, Global and CTV, could not survive the loss of big-budget American dramas, sitcoms, and reality shows if American networks created local Canadian affiliates. These networks, which have never demonstrated a strong commitment to Canadian programming, would have tremendous difficulty rebranding themselves as distinctly Canadian. If funding were cut to the CBC, it too would likely fold and its popular programming, notably *Hockey Night in Canada* and curling, would wind up on a newly created ESPN Canada or Fox Sports Canada channel. What is clear is that while Canadians claim to support Canadian culture, in the absence of a regulatory framework that enables and requires investment into indigenous culture, the audience would quickly disappear. This is not to suggest, therefore, that Canadians are merely pretending to care about diversity and accessibility on the airwaves. If anything, the idea here is to challenge a notion that cultural might makes right. To be sure, ratings for APTN may not be strong for non-native, or urban residents, but can arguments for its survival be based on economics alone? Even when arguments for cultural distinction are less clear-cut, as in the case of MuchMusic, for example, the fact remains that the channel has been crucial in the launching of successful Canadian acts such as Avril Lavigne or Barenaked Ladies, as well as more niche artists like Susan Aglukark.

The counter-suggestion – tighter regulation of the broadcasting industry with a greater emphasis on governmental participation – relies heavily upon a notion of Canada possessing a distinct and identifiable identity that must be preserved at all costs. Yet, contradictorily, if asked to define what that is, the stock answer tends to rely on the ubiquitous multicultural argument of openness, tolerance, and diversity. Even in a nationalist-oriented regulated market the widespread diversity of channels in Canada is unparalleled in the western world, including the United States. The argument could be made quite easily that this expansiveness defines Canadian broadcasting and is emblematic of our multicultural ethos. To suddenly shut down our borders isn't just economically and technologically unfeasible; it also undermines the spirit of Canadian culture as open and accepting of difference. Aside from the fact that restricting foreign television in Canada would be unpopular, there is ample evidence to suggest that the end result would amount to little more than an attack on Canada's core values, including multiculturalism.

In a previous era when many Canadians received only one television channel, the CBC, the network was widely held to promote a common good. With viewers across the country tuned to the same channel and watching the same entertainment, sports, and news sources, a common dialogue was encouraged that is often held to be synonymous with a healthy democracy. The myth of a common national dialogue was always false, however, particularly given the presence of French-language SRC in Quebec, a division that mitigated against the idea of a

common culture. As the country has grown and immigration expanded, subsequent additions to the range of broadcasters have served to
fracture and fragment the viewing audience so that few televisual
events manage to attract as much as 10 per cent of the nation at any
given time. For many Canadian nationalists, this is discouraging. Yet
it is evident that there never was a single audience in this country, except by compulsion. Further, the vision of CBC programmers in Toronto
rarely successfully united this multicultural country. The longing for
a single national broadcaster that can speak to all Canadians is a particular form of self-delusion, rooted in nostalgia for a vision of Canada
that never really existed, and which was championed to the cultural
exclusion of millions of citizens. The continuity of this myth is a troubling symptom of a lack of respect for diversity.

The rhetoric of choice mobilized by the cable industry stands in
contrast to the nationalist rhetoric utilized by broadcasters. However,
both are ultimately scarily similar in their insistence on depicting the
issue in terms of Canada's historic relationship to the United States
rather than our potential future as a global leader in a radically transformed mediascape. The CCTA maintains that its focus on competition
is "consumer driven" and pushes for greater levels of technological
convergence (telephone, cable, internet) that could then be managed
by cable companies as consumers integrate entertainment and communications technologies over digital networks. The fear, according
to the cable industry, is that, if the government fails to promote these
forms of convergence, consumers will simply use new technologies to
bypass Canadian systems entirely. CAB, on the other hand, observes
that the cable industry has used its near-monopoly powers to bully
broadcasters and limit consumer choice. Nonetheless, while both
broadcasters and the cable industry suggest that their policy priorities are what would most benefit individual consumers, it is clear that
they share a common antipathy to the broadcasting model that most
Canadians strongly favour, true à la carte options with an eye on plu-
ralism and diversity. That is, a globalized outlook that effectively ends
the American obsession that has plagued the country since the first
signal was broadcast. It is true that such a model would undermine
the Canadian broadcasting industry as it currently exists, resulting

in a period of great economic uncertainty and even collapse for some companies. It would also create a much smaller economy of scale as Canadian television would be designed effectively to no longer serve a mass audience, but a plurality of fractured, multivocal communities coordinated in a state of flux or disjuncture that embraces difference as both a cultural and political value. Yet, the chances of the television industry and regulatory agency pushing this agenda are almost nil, proving that, rhetoric aside, the primary concern facing the television industry remains maximizing shareholder value through captured audiences. Platitudes of Canadian cultural sovereignty are merely fodder in this regime. It protects the industry by preventing television from becoming a truly public space in which to enact cultural citizenship and keeps it locked down in its traditional place as a debased form of consumer passivity.

CHAPTER TWO: P

,RAMMING

Ashort article in the April 3, 2004, issue of *TV Guide* by Ben Mulroney encapsulates the current state of Canadian television programming. Mulroney, the son of the former prime minister and host of CTV's celebrity infotainment show *eTalk Daily*, describes his successes as an interviewer on the red carpet at the Academy Awards, which was broadcast by ABC and carried live in Canada by CTV. Mulroney writes: "Sandwiched between Joan Rivers and Roger Ebert, CTV's position on the carpet was better than ever. We took advantage of the backlog of stars waiting to talk with the big American outlets, and gave Canadians what I thought was a truly star-packed hour" (Mulroney 2004). The image of the Canadian broadcaster gratefully picking up the scraps from American networks says much about how success is defined for Canadian television. Mulroney ends with an anecdote intended to display Canadian moxie in the face of such obvious domination by American broadcasters. Apparently due to the Herculean efforts of his team, they managed to secure an exclusive interview with Renée Zellweger. "If you're wondering how that situation came to pass," says Mulroney, "here it is: we begged. My talented and dedicated producer got down on her knees and begged Renée not to turn her back on Canada" (Mulroney 2004). This is a similarly apt image, Canadian television as a beggar on the global stage, prostrate at the feet of American celebrity culture.

If Mulroney's fond reminiscences make Canadian television appear somewhat desperate, this is likely because it is often difficult to find bright spots on the English-Canadian television landscape. While it is worth looking in greater depth at contemporary shows that have earned a certain measure of success, such as CTV's *Corner Gas* and *Canadian Idol*, CBC's *The Greatest Canadian*, and the long-running *Degrassi* franchise, the fact remains that few Canadian dramatic or entertainment shows are watched in large numbers, and American programs dominate the ratings. In the spring of 2006, for example, the most popular entertainment programs on Canadian television were all American: *CSI, American Idol, CSI: Miami, Survivor, Desperate Housewives, Grey's Anatomy, The Amazing Race, House,* and *Criminal Minds. Corner Gas,* placing thirteenth on the list, was the only Canadian entertainment show in the top twenty. And while many point to the success of *Canadian Idol* as evidence that Canadians will watch their own, its success came during the late summer months, not during the regular season against the full-range of American competition. The ratings for popular television shows in Canada demonstrate not only that there is little difference between this country and the United States, but also that Canadians have few programming options other than major American network fare and smaller-scale Canadian productions.

The usual arguments for or against Canadian programs are often used to foster a division between what is deemed good for Canadians and what Canadians actually like. This is, of course, tied to television's historic reputation as a mass medium that is devoid of any edifying qualities. Thus, more than anything else, the anxiety over Canadian programming is deeply tied to notions of television as an inherently lowbrow medium that could, if suitably linked with good national values, be legitimated in terms of its service to the state, rather than through its aesthetic content. This is evident in the way that the industry has been regulated and monitored by successive governments since the earliest days of broadcasting. Further, it is one of the reasons why many studies on Canadian television focus more on the broadcasting system itself than on how that system is used, experienced, and valued by viewers on an everyday basis. When actual television programs do become the subject of debate, it is often in the form of a culturally nationalist outcry over the propensity of Canadians to watch American shows not only as a threat to sovereignty but also as a sign of plain poor taste. As Tracey and Redal argue, the viewing patterns of Canadians undermine the traditional rhetoric of our cultural distinction not just by demonstrating what we as a nation are not, but more troublingly, by clearly pointing out what we are: a nation that watches *America's Funniest Home Videos* in even greater proportional numbers than Americans (1995, 306). Attempts to rescue television from the American clutches through various political interventions ranging from quotas to programming funds are not necessarily illegitimate or a waste of taxpayers' money. They are, however, a rather ineffectual mask for the actual, unarticulated problem that has been present from the earliest days of television, which is the fear that it is a debased, populist medium beyond saving.

It should be stated here that the conception of Canada as merely a satellite of the American television marketplace is not entirely accurate. For one thing, Canada has many channels producing Canadian content that are simply not available in the United States. From this perspective, one could argue that Canada is the American broadcasting regime with a number of additional channels, or AmericaPlus. At the same time, however, a large number of American channels are denied to Canadians by the CRTC, ranging from MTV to The Disney Channel. Insofar as these channels are desirable to some Canadian viewers, Canadian broadcasting is experienced as AmericaMinus. To remain at this level of discussion, however, is to miss a broader point: Canada continues to define its television in direct reference to one other national market, the United States, rather than in terms of a far more expansive global culture. Even though Canada is the second largest exporter of television programs, very few Canadian stations provide the same kind of access to programming from other foreign markets (Tinic 2005, 159). Furthermore, what is available is usually on specialty "ethnic" or foreign-language services that are managed in such a way as to ensure very little cross-over audience except from those communities they are very narrowly designed to serve. Thus, the mainstream Canadian television market is limited to a triangulation of UK programming, which comprises only a tiny share and is usually marketed as prestige culture, U.S. programming, far and away the largest content provider and defined as commercialized product with a low-risk built-in audience, and Canadian shows which serve a primarily compensatory role filling in the gaps left behind by the other two.

In this sense, then, Canadian entertainment programming is not necessarily intended to be strictly for pleasure. As the self-congratulatory tone of Ben Mulroney suggests, even the most banal Canadian television event shoulders the burden of defining the nation through references to the United States – AmericaPlus or AmericaMinus. This narrow view of television's potential to mediate multiculturalism is borne out in the practices of the three major networks in Canada. CTV and Global expend most of their budget purchasing the rights to American programs for broadcast in Canada. CBC, on the other hand, with its focus on mostly Canadian television (with the notable exceptions of American movies and British soap operas), seeks to distinguish itself through appeals to traditional Canadian nationalism. Significantly, few of the CBC's programs, with the exception of NHL hockey, fare particularly well with the public. Nationalism, it seems, has its costs.

The struggle of the private broadcasters – primarily CTV and Global, but increasingly CHUM (since its purchase of Craig Broadcasting) and specialty channels like Alliance-Atlantis' Showcase – to fill their evenings with as many popular American shows as the CRTC will allow is standard in contemporary Canadian broadcasting. Shows like *American Dad*, *American Idol*, and *American Chopper* air unironically on Canadian channels with promotional bumpers touting "Canadian Television," to borrow CTV's tag-line. Broadcasters and the CRTC argue that this state of affairs is necessary so that Canadian networks can continue to produce high-quality Canadian shows like Ben Mulroney's *eTalk Daily*, but as American programs crowd out Canadian-produced material on the primetime schedules of Canadian broadcasters, it is difficult at times to imagine how this can possibly be the case. When Canadian programming consists of little more than inserting Ben Mulroney into cutaway segments during the Academy Awards, it is clear that the notion of Canadian content is increasingly bereft of meaning.

PRIMETIME SCHEDULING AND SIMULTANEOUS SUBSTITUTION

American shows are so important to Canadian television that they drive not only programming but also scheduling decisions, relegating Canadian dramas to the status of perennial bridesmaid. Ellen Baine, programming head of CHUM Television, notes that decisions for Canadian audiences cannot be made until the American schedules are settled: "For Canadians, the simulcasting is very important. You have to know what the Americans are doing" (in MacDonald 2004a). In fact, Canadian networks generally do not release their schedules until the American networks have finalized their own. The level of dependency is so acute that in 2000, when the American networks were delayed in publishing their schedules due to the uncertainty surrounding the dates of the debates in their presidential election, Canadian networks similarly followed suit ("New shows" 2000). The reason is simple. In order for Canadian networks to get optimum value for their purchases of American programs, they need to air the shows at the same time as they are aired in the United States. This allows the Canadian channel to use signal substitution to replace the American version of the show with the Canadian version on the American channel, thereby forcing Canadian viewers to watch Canadian advertisements and program promos. Simultaneous signal substitution is the very heart and soul of contemporary Canadian television, and the clearest indicator that economic models of national broadcasting are winning out over any cultural arguments. It is based on an industrial logic in which the audience merely serves a supporting role. In essence, the idea behind simultaneous substitution is that it is better for Canadians to watch *Law and Order* on a Canadian-owned station with Canadian advertisers than to watch it on an American NBC affiliate. Cultural arguments for "Canadian stories" go out the window here, leaving not much more than a vast network of protectionist regulations to prop up wealthy media industries with vague justifications about cultural sovereignty thrown in to silence critics.

It is difficult to imagine that Canadian television would exist in the form that it does today were it not for simultaneous substitution.

Removing this practice would seriously dilute the value of American programming on Canadian channels, reducing advertising revenues accordingly. The threat to revenue is felt so keenly that the CRTC has made substitution an integral aspect of broadcasting policy despite the fact that the practice annoys a large number of viewers. The problem is that it is often performed poorly, as when a signal change is made too late or too early, when a portion of a program is cut off by the Canadian broadcaster, or when promotional bumpers for programs are pre-empted. If this does not seem to be a particular hardship, it is nonetheless worth considering how this practice places the audience in a position of serving the broadcasters, rather than the other way around. While most of the time Canadians fume in silence, the issue comes to the forefront annually at the time of the NFL Super Bowl, where the commercials have become a part of the total entertainment package. As one of the most-watched events in television each year, the Super Bowl is increasingly a showcase for high-profile new advertisements. However, most American advertisers do not place these ads on Global, the Canadian broadcaster of the game. To the CRTC, this is a problem caused by American advertisers' unwillingness to spend money in Canada. For many Canadian viewers, it is a problem with a regulatory system designed to protect Canadian networks from competition. The CRTC publishes a standard statement about substitution and the Super Bowl on its website to offset the usual onslaught of viewer complaints. The justification is straightforward: "The use of simultaneous substitution means that more Canadians are watching Canadian stations, thus strengthening our broadcasting system as a whole.... With these increased revenues, Canadian broadcasters have a greater ability to make a financial contribution to the funding and production of Canadian television and to purchase quality programming" ("Signal substitution" 2004). Thus, according to the CRTC, if audiences don't watch the latest of Bell's beaver-themed advertisements then cultural sovereignty is undermined altogether.

As the CRTC states quite simply, the central argument in favour of simultaneous substitution is that the revenue generated by ads for American primetime programming can be used to subsidize less popular Canadian fare. This argument presumes that, in the absence of simultaneous substitution regulations, Canadian channels would offer no Canadian content. It sets up Canadian programming as a national duty. This is certainly a plausible position, particularly given the many efforts undertaken by Canadian private broadcasters to reduce or evade their licence obligations to provide Canadian content. In 2004/05, for example, private broadcasters spent $1.3 billion on acquiring programming, but only $587 million of that went to Canadian shows. And of that amount spent on indigenous programming, $369 million was for news and information shows, while only $86.6 million went to drama (CRTC 2006). However, the question remains: how would Canadian networks survive if the safety net of simultaneous substitution were removed? If American networks no longer needed to sell their shows to Canadian stations and could simply run them through their border affiliates – or through their own Canadian affiliates – it would be one less bureaucratic hurdle for them. That would significantly harm the easy economics of American programs for Canadian networks. Faced with this prospect, the networks could either stumble along with reduced revenues, or develop business strategies to win over Canadian viewers from American programs. Television producers and network chiefs tell us that this can't be done, but the example of Quebec, where all of the most popular shows are produced in the province and not merely imported from France, indicates that it is far from impossible. Indeed, there have been enough successes for Canadian television programs to suggest that, when pushed, network programmers can develop material that Canadians enjoy. However, they serve as much to highlight the problems facing Canadian television and its narrow outlook as they do to suggest alternatives routes of success. Indeed, by always looking over its shoulder to see what America is doing, the country fails to look ahead at other potential markets.

Finding original Canadian series on the primetime schedule is becoming more and more difficult. While CBC still holds itself as exemplifying all that is noble and uplifting about Canadian broadcasting, chinks have begun to show in its armour. The 2004/05 CBC schedule, for example, had less Canadian content than has appeared on the network in prime time in many years. While the network continues to boast that it offers a "mostly Canadian" schedule (Canadian

Press 2004), it nonetheless added the long-running British soap opera *Coronation Street* to its nightly primetime schedule. When their flagship Canadian program, *Hockey Night in Canada* was cancelled following the 2004/05 NHL lockout and the subsequent cancellation of the hockey season, CBC filled their Saturday nights with triple features of Hollywood movies, most of which, like Mel Gibson's *Braveheart*, had aired many times before on other stations. They had little else to offer in 2004 in terms of indigenous dramatic programming, other than the return of stalwarts such as *Da Vinci's City Hall* and *This is Wonderland*. Then, in March 2006, even those programs were cancelled. With scheduling decisions such as these, the CBC's ongoing commitment to Canadian content appeared limited to lip service to cultural nationalists. Friends of Canadian Broadcasting wrote to CBC president Robert Rabinovitch in October 2004, to suggest that the CBC replace NHL games with CHL games, thereby maintaining Canadian content, providing more national sports coverage, and exposing Canadians to other forms of hockey, instead of the increasingly American-dominated NHL. The CBC responded by noting that they did not hold the rights to broadcast CHL games, that reruns of older hockey games had fared poorly in the ratings, and, most importantly, that the turn to American movies is, as programming head Slawko Klymkiw noted, "not a cultural strategy; it's a revenue strategy" (Zelkovich 2004a). One month into the *Movie Night in Canada* experiment, the films were initially doing ratings comparable to those of the NHL broadcasts, averaging 1.1 million viewers in comparison to hockey's 1.2 million (MacDonald 2004b), further bolstering the economic argument for a protected national public broadcaster at the expense of any cultural justification.

Nonetheless, despite its failings, the CBC's commitment to distinctly Canadian programming still outpaces that of private broadcasters Global and CTV. Global, for example, ran only one Canadian-produced drama in 2005, *Zoe Busiek: Wild Card*, which features American star Joely Fisher and is set in Chicago. In November 2004, the network fired their Canadian programming heads and replaced them with Americans, leading many to wonder if their meagre commitment to Canadian programming would come under further attack (Davidson 2004). They got their answer three months later when the only Canadian dramatic series on their schedule was cancelled. Similarly, CTV announced a small number of new dramatic shows for the 2004/05 season, including *Robson Arms* and *Instant Star*, but did not immediately air them. All in all, it seemed clear in 2004 that Canadian dramas and sitcoms were not high priorities for Canada's broadcast networks nor has support subsequently rebounded. In fact, in 2006, CBC followed the example of Global and hired an American film producer, Fred Fuchs, to take over as the executive director of Arts and Entertainment Programming. When asked his opinion on what the CBC is doing right or wrong, he answered, "It's really too early for me to understand the complexities of all the issues" (Dixon 2006). In 1999 the networks were airing eleven Canadian-made hour-long primetime dramas, but by 2003/04 that number had declined to six (Gill 2004). One year later, two of these six were cancelled.

It is clear that the Canadian primetime schedule is driven not by the interests and desires of Canadians but by the trends and formulas of American networks. Very little risk is taken as both private and public broadcasters rely on programming that has already been tested and proven successful elsewhere. The example of reality television is indicative of Canadian broadcasters' dependency on America and their hesitancy to look beyond that north-south axis to build broadcasting alliances on a more truly global scale. Canadian private broadcasters have quickly snatched up American versions of reality shows with the same enthusiasm they have shown for network dramas. Describing the 2004/05 schedule, for example, Loren Mawhinney, head of Global's Canadian programming, said: "People seem to be very very interested in reality still. It's very hard for a Canadian series to drive the audience in the same way" ("Networks" 2004). Indeed, Global was so tied to the increasingly faltering reality bandwagon that they proposed an all-reality television diginet to the CRTC, and the CBC hired Pia Marquand to be a "reality guru" (Gill 2004).

The rise of reality programming isn't just a problem of Canadian broadcasters continuing to poach American programming. It also raises questions about just how innovative broadcasters are in trying to create a unique Canadian television culture that embraces our multicultural heritage. The big lie of reality television is that it is an example of lowbrow American programming. In fact, many of the most popular shows were adapted from original European shows. Thus, if anything, it appears that American broadcasters are far more aware of global television trends than we are. If Canadian television producers are constantly on the lookout for affordable programming alternatives, why did it take American producers to borrow the low-budget *Survivor* concept from the Swedes, the *Big Brother* concept from the Dutch, and the *Pop Idol* concept from the British? Alexandra Gill implies in *The Globe and Mail* that Canada, with its focus on ennobling and educational television, simply could not conceptualize the lowbrow reality fare: "For the most part, however, we could hold our heads high and tell ourselves this was just another big, fat, obnoxious trend tempting us from afar. Other than Ben Mulroney and his merry Canadian Idols, reality was not the type of television we were very good at making" (Gill 2004). The timing for Canada to leap into the reality waters only after it had proven itself in America, however, suggests not a snob-induced lethargy, but rather a failure of creativity and openness to alternative programming models that keep other second-tier market nations afloat. Maureen Parker, executive director of the Writer's Union of Canada observes, "There's no risk, no gamble, no investment. They're just purchasing formats from other countries" (in Gill 2004). However, it isn't even from multiple countries, given that Canadian broadcasters don't try a format that hasn't been proven in the United States. Thus, for example, the networks purchase *Big Brother* from CBS but not the original – and far more racy – European version.

Of course, not all Canadian reality shows are straightforward derivatives of American vehicles; some actually try to give a distinctly Canadian angle. A case in point is *Making the Cut*, CBC's thirteen-part reality show about hockey players attempting to win a spot in the training camps of the six Canadian NHL teams. *The Globe and Mail's* television critic, John Doyle, praised the show as representative of everything that is right and true about Canadian culture. Doyle writes, "Gorgeously made and rich in Canadian archetypes, it's the perfect expression of who we are"; that it is "all so abundant in scenes and situations that strike a Canadian chord"; and that it is "about destiny, determination and luck. It's also vastly entertaining and very much ours" (Doyle 2004). For Doyle, *Making the Cut* is a perfect exemplar of the values and traditions that differentiate Canada from the United States and the rest of the world. Indeed, he goes so far as to equate the show with the very source of Canadian cultural life: "We can speculate forever about why hockey has such depth of meaning in the collective soul. A rough but still-elegant game played on the ice by men wearing layers of protection, often at night, is partly primordial in significance – it about the need to defeat the ice, cold and darkness, and frolic in the face of the elements that could defeat us if we allowed ourselves to be diminished by them. It's about surviving. It's about defeating death" (Doyle 2004). Despite such poetry, the show did not apparently speak to Canadians as strongly as it spoke to John Doyle. Ratings for the show started poorly and dropped over time, pulling in slightly more than 400,000 viewers on Tuesday nights and trailing even other Canadian shows airing at the same time on CTV ("Sports reality" 2004). Global's programming head, Alan Ivars, suggested that the show may have been undermined by the lack of a compelling story. He states, "What drives reality shows are the characters. If the characters aren't compelling, it doesn't matter what the backdrop is – hockey or boxing or wrestling – it's not going to work. The reason shows like *Making the Cut* aren't working is that they're focusing more on the backdrop than on the characters" ("Sports reality" 2004). That backdrop is the aching need to prove its Canadianness by doling out every stereotype that cultural nationalists crave and insisting that we recognize ourselves in a picture that looks increasingly less like the country in which we all live.

Of course, criticizing shows like *Making the Cut* for wallowing in homogenous cultural stereotypes is one thing, but the more important issue is to explore the particular ways that Canadian shows mobilize nationalist tropes in order to prove their civic value and justify the millions of public support dollars given to shore up a production industry that seems to make products that the country doesn't really want. If the goal is to create some kind of a sense of common national character through the various forms of the television medium, then most people would argue that Canadian broadcasting has failed, and they would correctly point to the lack of programs and weak ratings for the few that do exist. However, there are many cases in which Canadian television organizes itself for survival, if not outright success. Canadians tend to associate the key problems surrounding national television with dramatic or entertainment production, but the best successes tend to happen in the realms of informational programming. This is borne out in a recent study by Statistics Canada that notes that Canadians watch news and sports almost as frequently as they do comedy and drama – with each occupying 34.4 and 36.2 per cent of viewing time respectively. However, when the percentage of viewing time is broken down between Canadian and non-Canadian programming, the numbers change dramatically. Of all comedy and drama programming, only 18 per cent of it is Canadian. By contrast, out of the total news and sports viewing, 70 per cent is Canadian (Statistics Canada 2005). Yet, dramatic programming is still considered the pinnacle of television achievement, at least on the cultural level, despite the fact that it is frequently an economic loser. More importantly, it is the primary driver of cultural nationalists who argue for broadcasting policies that place a premium on telling Canadian stories.

Nonetheless, the tendency has been in the past for scholars and critics to deftly avoid looking concretely at Canadian dramatic or entertainment shows and focus instead on policy, history, and technology issues. Part of the reason for this is that so few shows enter into a kind of public consciousness where there is enough common knowledge to discuss them in any depth. However, we feel there is another more problematic reason why television content is so downplayed. It has something to do with the nagging sense that television isn't worthy of lengthy, introspective debate because of its inherently populist appeal. In other words, while the idea of the CBC is well worth exploring in depth, *The Royal Canadian Air Farce*, one of its longest-running shows, is not.

ENTERTAINMENT PROGRAMMING: WHAT MAKES A STORY CANADIAN?

Interestingly, what is not often openly acknowledged is that the backbone of Canadian television production is cheaply produced syndication shows designed for the international market. This is a far cry from the noble intentions of governmental support agencies that are intent on bolstering quality shows for a distinctly Canadian audience. Anyone who has been channel flipping and stumbled over such shows as *StarGate SGI*, *Relic Hunter*, or *PSI Factor* is seeing the most abundant fruits of the Canadian television production sector. Very few of these shows have any kind of Canadian indicators, and most, like *Sue Thomas: FBEye* are clearly set in the United States. In many ways, these shows are the logical outcomes of what producers in the United States call "runaway productions": American-funded programs that take advantage of low Canadian currency exchange, cheaper labour, and significant tax incentives to produce their shows here. *X-Files*, the legendary cult show that aired on Fox from 1993 to 2002, is the most successful of these, but as American specialty cable networks become more invested in developing original programming, the lure of lower production overhead brings them north of the border. Between runaway productions and the syndication market, the Canadian television experience can tend to slide into a kind of parlour game in which viewers try to guess the filming locale that is meant to stand in for Chicago, or pick out Canadian actors in bit roles. Both Pat Mastroianni (Joey Jeremiah from the long-running *Degrassi* franchise) and Nicholas Campbell (*Da Vinci's Inquest*), for example, had small guest star turns on the short-lived ESPN show *Playmakers*, which followed tne ups and downs of an American professional football team, but which was filmed at Toronto's SkyDome. Supporters of the syndication and runaway production model argue, quite legitimately, that such shows are important to the economic life of Canada's cultural and entertainment sectors. They shore up an industry that employs thousands of artists, technicians, tradespeople, and professionals, making possible more risky, creative ventures when the time allows. Furthermore, as Tinic points out, they also serve as a kind of frontier resistance to the centrist model of "quality Canadian programming" by offering production companies outside of the Toronto-dominated national market a chance to set their sights on international markets instead. Of course, as in almost all aspects of Canadian television, a sense of failure is built into this model, whereby the "real" Canadian shows that cultural nationalists lobby for, ones that showcase prestige performances, groundbreaking stories, or explicitly foster a sense of national identity, are assumed to not have the same drawing power as a show about a deaf FBI agent and her dog. Thus, in the name of middlebrow nationalism, these shows craftily keep their Canadian credentials in the shadows. They may be important to the Canadian television economy, but they're the dirty little secret of Canadian television culture that is supposed to be above the populist pandering that supposedly characterizes American commercial product.

When networks create an explicitly Canadian show for the national market, they want to make sure you know it, often by throwing the word "Canadian" into the title, or by deliberately, almost archly avoiding any kind of glitzy polish in favour of a more down to earth and "like real life" look. Perhaps two of the most popular dramatic series that wear their Canadianism on their sleeves are the sleeper hit *Corner Gas* and the perennial favourite *Degrassi*, now in its fourth incarnation as *The Next Generation*. Both air on CTV, although *Degrassi* got its start on CBC in 1982, and both have garnered respectable ratings and critical raves, particularly by Canadian standards.

Corner Gas is a half-hour sitcom following the classic fish-out-of-water formula, in which Lacey Burrows moves from Toronto to the tiny Saskatchewan town of Dog River to take over her aunt's diner. There she is befriended by the owner of the only gas station in town, who is played by Brent Butt, the creator of the show, as one of the few non-eccentrics dotting the rather barren landscape. Together the two observe with bemused pleasure the antics of their friends, family, and neighbours in this isolated farming community. Certain stock Canadian characters are present, including the native police chief and the young hoser. Storylines are built around small themes of everyday life, such as when Lacey discovers that the entire town believes the rather doughy Brent is a hot stud. The pace of the show is deliberately low-key, and the humour is ironic and observational as it knowingly plays on standard national stereotypes and then winks smartly at the expectations of the audience for a Canadian show. In that sense, then, *Corner Gas* succeeds in fulfilling nationalist tropes of distinct Canadian stories, but it creates a sense of concordance with the audience that these tropes are tired, paternalistic, and sometimes even downright insulting. At the same time, its sympathy for rural life is explicit, and its intentionally non-network look and feel, even as it borrows liberally from an American genre, suggests that this is not a show for anyone other than Canadians. Thus, it helps to perpetuate an artificial divide between those Canadian dramatic series designed for the global market that consciously hide their identity in order to fit with a perceived homogenous standard and are almost embarrassing in their low production values and the more inward-looking form of homogeneity that preserves cultural and financial investment for a show that presents a bucolic although slightly cynical small-town Canada that resonates with all the common indicators of how we are like America, but not.

Degrassi: The Next Generation also plays with these strategies of distinction from American programs, and claims a position of prestige against its most obvious competitors like the Fox shows *The O.C.* and its predecessor *Beverly Hills 90210*. Unlike these shows, which feature older and beautiful actors playing teenagers who drive sports cars, live in Malibu mansions, and wear high-fashion designer wear to school, *Degrassi* has always characterized itself as being a honest, unflinching look at growing up. Much ink has been spilled over the years distinguishing it from its American counterparts, noting the gawkiness of some of the actors as they pass puberty, and their blossoming on screen over successive seasons and series. If anything, since CTV revived the franchise with a new cast of characters based on the now-grown-up characters from *The Kids from Degrassi, Degrassi Junior High*, and *Degrassi High*, the show has been criticized for not being gritty enough. Certainly production quality is noticeably higher and the soap opera storylines have been intensified as emotional plots involving issues like school shootings, sex parties, and date rape are played out quickly and dramatically. The nostalgia factor also runs high as characters from the former series provide the framework for the new show, especially the all-too-formulaic family of Emma, the now-teenage daughter of Spike/Christine, and her step-father Snake/Archie who is also her home room teacher and was Spike's school-days friend. Both parents were featured players in the original series and their friends, in particular the popular romantic couple Joey and Caitlin, have also been written into the storyline. The cult-like success of *Degrassi* has been bolstered by such high-profile fans as Kevin Smith, the indy director of *Dogma* and *Mall Rats*, who directed and guest-starred in a three-episode arc for the 2004/05 season. There was also a lengthy feature in the *New York Times Magazine* heralding it as "tha Best Teen TV N da WRLD!" for its ability to capture the reality of high school life, and its deft balance between educational and entertainment television (Neihart 2005). Originally syndicated in the United States by PBS but now showing on the specialty children's network Nickelodeon, *Degrassi* has spawned a fiercely loyal audience in the United States, a point that is made frequently in reviews and profiles of the show. Interestingly, what is often referenced is the idea that the show demonstrates the higher level of sophistication of Canadian audiences, who can handle such controversial storylines as abortion while those episodes had to be pre-empted in the States. Thus, again, the success of *Degrassi* as a distinctly Canadian show is defined through its ability to emulate American television but only because it is more edifying, less commercial.

Canadian dramatic television successes like *Corner Gas* and *Degrassi: The Next Generation* point to the way that popular Canadian television shows are generally assessed along strictly nationalist terms and in relation to the American market, and seen in terms of the way that they register similarities to and differences from similar American material. The same is true, only more so, for the recent ventures into reality television. Two of the more successful Canadian programs are actually borrowed concepts from the UK and the United States. *Canadian Idol* is a franchise of *American Idol*, which in turn borrowed the concept from the UK's *Pop Idol*. More conspicuously nationalistic, *The Greatest Canadian* aired on CBC and encouraged audiences to vote for their favourite Canadian personality. It was adapted from the BBC series *Great Britons*, which has subsequently been franchised around the world.

Produced by CTV and hosted by celebrity hound Ben Mulroney, *Canadian Idol* is one of the most popular Canadian shows in history, claiming the number one spot in the ratings for the finale of its second season. Although the model for the show had existed in Europe for years prior, Canada waited until it had been successfully tested as an American brand before launching its own franchise. The structure of the show is simple. A panel of semi-celebrity judges, including minor 1980s pop star Sass Jordan, tours the country auditioning hopeful singing sensations. For the most part, one type of music is preferred, the "blue-eyed soul" of adult contemporary R&B, with occasional splashes of new country. The finalists return to Toronto for a series of weekly singing competitions that are voted on electronically by the viewing audience through special telephone and web services. The winner receives a recording contract and a cross-country tour. As the ultimate branch-plant program, *Canadian Idol* certainly demonstrates the worst that can happen when the homogenizing influences of globalization take hold of the airwaves. The show is numbingly formulaic, much like contemporary pop radio, and the hyperactive antics of Ben Mulroney only heighten the feeling that not much is really going on here. However, it is incredibly successful not only in ratings but also in drumming up a sense of regional pride that then reverberates on a national level as the show nears its finale. Idol audition dates are widely publicized events that garner enormous attention by local media. While the bulk of the show takes place in Toronto, the weeks leading up are set in some of the smaller towns in the country like Medicine Hat, Alberta, which was home to the second season winner, Kalan Porter. In that sense, then, the hopes and dreams of the contestants are mirrored in that of the country as a whole, to somehow be bigger and better than they really are.

Interestingly, two key moments in the series highlight this anxiety to exceed expectations that is reflected in both singers and the country as a whole. In the first season, the American producers created a spin-off called *International Idol* in which the winners from various national versions of the show competed for the supreme top spot. The show is mostly noteworthy for the fact that the odds-on favourite, American Kelly Clarkson, was blown out of the competition by the gap-toothed Norwegian winner, Kurt Nilsen, who departed from the formula by singing "Beautiful Day" by the Irish arena rock band U2. This is worth pointing out to show how in even the most egregious example of Americanized globalization, small glimmers of resistance persistently shine through. It's also important because the Canadian contestant, Ryan Malcolm, revealed himself as being the least distinguished from the American model. Many of the countries showed some small measure of distinction by fielding contestants who didn't necessarily look, sound, act, or sing like a star-factory American singer. Malcolm, by contrast, was noticeable by his carefully manufactured image, which completely fit within the mould set by the American version of the show – only duller. This bold AmericaMinus effort resulted in rather dismal rankings in the international competition. Malcolm was number one for Canadian voters, but his only other top three position was from the pan-Arabic region, and he finished sixth overall.

Perhaps chastened by their attempt to out-America *American Idol* in the first season, the second season of *Canadian Idol* decided to put a much more explicitly Canadian spin on the show, at least for one night. It featured a special all-Canadian evening of songs, in particular a tribute to the legendary folk singer Gordon Lightfoot, who was enjoying a resurgence of interest in the media due to a near-brush with death in 2002. CTV was not above using that fact to sell the episode, stating in its own online news story, "The six young singers left on *Canadian Idol* honoured a living Canadian legend – one who came perilously close to becoming a dead one" ("Idol hopefuls" 2004). Contestants were coached by Lightfoot into various tableau settings for renditions of such classics as "The Canadian Railroad Trilogy." The ability of the *Canadian Idol* producers to generate media buzz is nearly unparalleled in the country, as again the media rushed to report on this unique, quintessentially patriotic moment. In an interview on *eTalk Daily*, Lightfoot himself played up the nationalist angle by noting how *Canadian Idol* can help lead to recording contracts for young singers and offering up the final summation that the show "is important for Canada" ("Canadian Idol" 2004). However, it was only one moment and a fleeting one at that, as the next week they returned to the pat formula of primarily American Top 40 hits sung in flat, booming voices.

It is, perhaps, too easy to take potshots at *Canadian Idol* for its dull, homogenous programming, its unabashed borrowing of an American model with just enough flag-waving thrown in to pass itself off as an original Canadian series. In many ways, it represents the worst of Canadian television and offers renewed proof of why a national public broadcaster is so essential. However, CBC's major event of the 2004/05 season, around which it built the remainder of its schedule, closely followed the formula set out by reality show franchises, only set the flag waving to a frenetic pace. *The Greatest Canadian* was trumpeted as the thinking person's *Canadian Idol*. The series relied on votes cast by Canadians to establish a list of the fifty greatest Canadians to have ever lived, and then produced one-hour advocacy documentaries about each of the top ten finalists. The series concluded with ten celebrity advocates debating the merits of their nominees in front of a live studio audience, and, on the following night, the countdown to the final winner. The show was seen by television critics as an effort on the part of the CBC to deliberately shed their dour, stodgy image by undertaking a show that would be hip and edgy, yet still educational and ennobling. The fact that the concept was taken whole cloth from British television's *Great Britons* series was also reassuring as it not only mitigated any risk by going with a known successful formula, but also had that tinge of colonial respectability that BBC shows tend to bring. In promoting the show, and the newly hip status of the CBC in general, Slawko Klymkiw, the executive director of network programming, told *The Globe and Mail*: "We're showing a sense of humour and a populist side. CBC can't be serious and stodgy all the time" (Allemang 2004). Following this lead, producer Mark Starowicz argued that the show was the CBC's effort to proselytize the importance of Canadian history in a format that would be appealing to young people. By including MuchMusic VJ George Stroumboulopoulos (who inked a permanent deal with CBC Newsworld while the show was on the air) and ex-Hole bassist Melissa Auf der Mar as celebrity hosts for the finale, it was hoped that Canadian history could be made palatable to viewers who might otherwise avoid such an exercise. Starowicz claimed, "Our job is to proselytize knowledge and art. It's in the Broadcasting Act. And the vast majority seem to appreciate this form – it's reaching a younger demographic" (Allemang 2004).

Starowicz' invocation of the broadcasting act to promote a reality television show may seem odd at first but it says much about the current condition of the public broadcaster as television becomes increasingly regulated according to economic rather than cultural goals. His assessment of the CBC's obligations is correct, but for the typical viewer sitting down on any given night to watch television, almost wholly irrelevant. The moral obligation to support Canadian culture and the desire of the viewer to be entertained on any given evening often exist in stark contrast to one another. The CBC, granted millions of tax dollars annually to present Canadians to themselves, has become the most important agency in terms of creating and disseminating Canadian culture, and its every move is scrutinized by supporters, critics, and, most importantly, governments. The Greatest Canadian, therefore, as an attempt to be both serious and irreverent at the same time, highlights the anxieties that plague Canadian culture. Neither genuinely elitist nor truly populist, the show signals the inherently middlebrow intentions of the CBC, even as the traditional model of creating programs that will enrich television for the greater good of the state is beginning to show its age.

While initially the show performed well, the lack of a strong celebrity culture in Canada led to weakening ratings as each successive hour-long profile of the top ten finalists dragged on. Further, it's hard to imagine how a show on Frederick Banting, the inventor of insulin, or Lester B. Pearson, the Nobel Prize-winning former prime minister, could be made riveting. Yet, audiences did return in slightly smaller-than-expected numbers for the final unveiling in which a host of media, political, and entertainment figures debated the merits of each contestant while final votes were counted and socialist politician Tommy Douglas, the father of medicare, was declared the winner. The CBC also declared themselves winners for attracting a more youthful audience and generating more buzz than they had in a long, long time (although only a small fraction of the media coverage generated by Canadian Idol). However, the show is clearly a one-time event, as the idea of a second season is impossible. It seems as if the CBC does not want to sully itself in the reality waters too much lest it lose its privileged status as the haven for high-minded cultural achievements.

Some key themes can be derived from these four shows. The most obvious is the way that they each serve a compensatory role in their claims to offer up something distinctly Canadian but are still defined by their relationship to similar American (or in the case of *The Greatest Canadian*, British) programs. What is also important about their success, though, is how keenly aware each of them is of its lack of originality and its doggedly national outlook both in terms of ratings and the generation of critical media attention. Economically and culturally, then, Canadian television programming continues to look for the surefire formula for success on territorial grounds. The problem with Canadian television filling this compensatory role is that it is attempting to work within two modes that are often deemed antithetical: the popular and the prestigious. The situation is exacerbated by the contradictions also inherent in using culturalist arguments to justify a largely economic infrastructure. Ben Mulroney's claims that his exclusive interview with Zellweger serves as some kind of celebrity version of 'capture the flag' shows how populist Canadian programming seeks to both mimic the look and feel of American shows while still mitigating the guilt Canadian audiences are presumed to experience for going for glitz over substance. The alternative to this form of programming is the prestige show explicitly designed to offer a culturally, socially, and intellectually edifying experience, but which is not necessarily always entertaining. These are usually television movies or mini-series that have very explicit Canadian themes and recognizable actors and can be said to offer additional political or social value in addition to their function as national culture. There is, however, a third generalizable form of Canadian entertainment programming that operates somewhere between the populist and the prestigious and is best known for its ironic playfulness with myths of Canadian television. Usually, this kind of program is a humour or sketch comedy series that openly mocks the arch sincerity of the cultural nationalist argument even while slyly signalling that the audience knows they are in fact better than America. The prestige and the ironically populist, therefore, serve as the two poles of establishing a sense of Canadian distinction vis-à-vis the United States. This was clearly seen at the 2004 Gemini awards.

Celebrating the best of English Canadian television production, the 2004 Gemini awards highlight a number of issues surrounding the current state of television. The big winner of the night was *Human Cargo*, a CBC co-produced mini-series that won seventeen awards, including those for writing, direction, and best mini-series or TV movie. In many ways, the low-rated series is a quintessential Canadian prestige project. The well-known stage and screen veteran, Kate Nelligan, stars as a Canadian immigration board member who must confront her own racism as she listens to the personal stories of immigrants, while her daughter volunteers on the front lines of a humanitarian crisis in Africa. Revolving around issues raised by racism, immigration policy, and official multiculturalism, *Human Cargo* is a classic example of how dramatic television programming can be used to reflect upon important issues facing Canada as a nation with an increasingly global outlook but from a resolutely nationalist perspective. Further, the show is bolstered by the presence of a raft of well-regarded Canadian actors supporting Nelligan, including Nicholas Campbell from *Da Vinci's Inquest*, Cara Pifko, the star of *This is Wonderland*, and R. H. Thomson, a feature actor in numerous Canadian prestige television shows and mini-series, including *Road to Avonlea* and *Trudeau*.

The producers of *Human Cargo* took pains to ensure that their project remained distinctly Canadian not only culturally but also economically. However, this decision is expressed ambivalently, beginning first on a rather patriotic note and then ending in a state of defeat and anxiety. In an interview in the *Vancouver Sun*, co-producer Brian McKeown notes, "It's a little Canadian production. It's very much a Vancouver production. Two little Vancouver companies have done this and we did it as 100-per-cent Canadian. The trick there, of course, was that we couldn't spend any more than 25 per cent of our budget outside the country. If we went offside on that our whole financial structure would collapse. We were totally, totally boxed in" (McNamara 2004). Thus, creating Canadian television is framed as an issue of working within funding guidelines to build a success, rather than as a risk-taking production that does whatever is necessary to achieve an aesthetic goal. This sense of defiant defeatism also exists in the way the show was publicized as an obvious tough sell to audiences. As the *Calgary Herald* points out, "stories with Third World themes can be a hard sell in a medium that doesn't usually look much beyond domestic borders" (Atherton 2004). Other reviews noted that it was "a dense slog" (Kohanik 2005) but recommended it as the kind of television that Canadians should be making and watching. Even the mini-series' director, after winning a record seven Geminis, said rather pointedly, "It's important to tell Canadian stories but in these days of the United States of Canada and Jesusland, it's also important to look at stories about Canada and the world" ("A nice haul" 2004). Thus, even in a production that very deliberately separated itself from American visions both in terms of content and financing, the idea of presenting Canada within the world is defined against its perpetually present rival, rather than through the more complex multicultural lens that *Human Cargo* is supposed to be exploring.

The winner of the Gemini award for Best Comedy series offered a stark contrast to the kind of ennobling discourse surrounding *Human Cargo*. Showcase's *Trailer Park Boys* beat out traditional CBC fare such as the long-running perennial *Red Green Show*, seven-time winner *This Hour Has Twenty-Two Minutes*, and the critically acclaimed *The Newsroom*, as well as CTV's popular success story *Corner Gas* (which took the prize the next year). In winning the award, *Trailer Park Boys* became not only the first cable show to be so honoured, but the first non-CBC produced comedy to take home the Gemini in the comedy category. The win, therefore, signalled a shift in the thinking about the nature of "quality" comedy in Canada. *Trailer Park Boys*, which follows the profane exploits of three losers in a Halifax trailer park, is an edgy and family-hostile show that has gathered a cult following on cable and on DVD. It deliberately sets out to exploit the limitations of Canadian television production by using a mockumentary format that allows for visibly cheap production values and makes the small budget part of the overall feel of the show. Exported to the United States in censored form by BBC America, the show exemplifies the compensatory model from a global position. Its resolutely lowbrow premise and crass humour would seem well at home on the American networks, nestled between *COPS* and *Wife Swap*. However, it airs on the arts-oriented channel Showcase in Canada and is mediated internationally through that stalwart of good taste, BBC, suggesting that the show is well aware that it is playing lowbrow but is in fact much smarter than that. With its love-it-or-hate-it appeal, *Trailer Park Boys* is the type of controversial award winner that Canada has rarely favoured, a Gemini winner that many would consider a possible worst-of nominee.

How is it that a show that exemplifies the traditional, nationalist model of Canadian broadcasting and a show that essentially thumbs its nose at such ideals could both earn the highest honours? The answer may lie within Linda Hutcheon's notion of the Canadian postmodern, in which the nation has conveniently skipped a step and is no longer even worried about achieving a state of unity or coherence in its national culture. Instead, a postmodern approach in which that very goal is doubled in on itself, in which it is both identified and named but then challenged and undermined simultaneously, may be taking precedence (1988, 6). In other words, what *Human Cargo* offers is the unsmiling, straightforward and sincere version of a myth of Canada that may well be desirable but comes with so much elitist baggage that it needs to be taken down a peg or two by also embracing *Trailer Park Boys*. At the same time, it is possible that this double-edged sword of Canadian television also reflects Canada's anxiety to be fully modern, and not its exuberance at bypassing this stage of evolution altogether. As Dorland and Charland argue, the persistent theme of survival in Canadian art and culture implies a project of Canada that is just struggling to stay alive, but not really expecting to ever be satisfactorily completed (2002, 50). This leaves a mildly bitter taste of irony tinged with a reflexive kind of cynicism in even the noblest of national building enterprises. Postmodern or modern-in-waiting, these two very different theories both provide some way of bridging the two halves into an alternative kind of whole: not a smooth, intact circle, but a concatenation of different and distorted shapes that together comprise an alternative view of the nation not from a modernist standpoint of cultural sovereignty but as one that is willing if not eager to open up its borders to multiple flows of cultural ideas and vantage points. What the example of Canadian dramatic and entertainment programming has shown, however, is that in the fervent desire to define and shape television according to a deeply ambivalent and contradictory relationship to the United States, Canada has succeeded only in blocking out other promising cultural relationships and preventing this flow from happening.

To a certain degree, the economic realities of the mediascape are changing the situation for Canadian television production. The global broadcasting market is thirsty for content, and new models of financing make possible international cooperation between multiple countries. There is enormous potential for Canadian dramatic programming that abandons the nationalist dream of unity and identity and considers a globalized outlook of heterogenous culture. Certainly, there is room on the dial, and old arguments of media scarcity have an antiquated feel to them in the era of digital, satellite, and other seemingly endlessly expansive technologies. Ironically, again Canada can look to the United States for assurance that alternatives to the mass broadcasting network exist. Niche programs like *Trailer Park Boys* which air on specialty cable channels offer exciting new opportunities both economically and culturally. Smaller-scale production, shorter seasons, and lower budgets are necessities reflecting smaller audience share and lower market penetration. However, rather than seeing these as a problem, niche networks like HBO have put their resources into fewer shows that stand out not only in terms of quality but also in risk-taking and challenging the borders of television. While for the most part these risks have been in the form of sex and violence, they nonetheless present a challenge to the Canadian tendency to crank out low-quality syndication shows with the justification that they can't compete with American network production values. However, for a new model of Canadian television to really make an impact, it is critical that the focus cease to be so narrowly and resentfully on America. A multicultural approach to Canadian television on a global scale leapfrogs Canada over traditional broadcasting models based on nationalism, cultural sovereignty, and protectionist policies. There are glimmers that it may be happening already with the 2005 winner for best drama. *Sex Traffic*, about the slave trade between the former Soviet Union and western countries, was a co-production between a small Nova Scotia-based production company, the British stalwart Granada Television, and the CBC. While Hutcheon's arguments of a postmodern nation are controversial and challenged by many scholars of Canada, there is something promising there with regards to television that is worth considering. What if the hallmark of this nation was that it no longer was preoccupied with defining itself categorically and conclusively but was perpetually open to multiple cross-border flows of media and culture? In this way, there is no doubt that Canada has the potential to be an important leader in a new model of globalized broadcasting that is founded on principles of multiculturalism and heterogeneity.

RETURNING TO THE LOCAL: INFORMATION PROGRAMMING

Although we've painted a picture of a new Canadian television culture with near-utopian optimism, it is absolutely clear that it is not possible to simply trade a form of nationalism for a new form of globalization. To do so, even if it were possible, would be to fundamentally ignore a central function of television, which is local programming. And that requires a national infrastructure to support and maintain it. Dramatic and entertainment shows tend to be produced for the largest, therefore national and international, markets. Yet, as the StatsCan report shows, audiences in Canada are increasingly relying on television not for entertainment but for information (Statistics Canada 2005). It is little wonder, then, that some of the most successful Canadian shows are local news and sports broadcasts. The tendency of grey market satellite owners to maintain a Canadian basic cable subscription in order to receive local channels for news, sports, and weather is suggestive of the importance of local programming to television viewers. There is even a sizeable grey market satellite industry for ex-pat Canadians living in the United States (Colker 2004). It appears, then, that information programming, which is rarely discussed by cultural nationalists as a crucial element of the broadcasting field, is far more effective at creating a sense of national unity than any uplifting dramatic mini-series.

Nonetheless, what makes local programming so valuable isn't its doggedly nationalist character but its commitment to the community. Even nationally based services like Newsworld, TSN, and the Weather Network tailor their programming to fit the needs and interests of the different regions in the country. Moreover, when they do this, it is regarded as part of a process of strengthening regional connections across the country, rather than undermining national unity. Obviously, the weather in Edmonton is of little or no value to someone deciding whether or not to carry an umbrella in Halifax. However, the local orientation of information programming in news and sports does say something about the way that the vastly different regions of this country fit together to create the conditions for a far more global, multicultural outlook on its national character. As Richard Collins argues, the traditional sense of Canada as in a perpetual state of identity crisis can actually be positive in that it allows for disruptions and disturbances in the cultural fabric with minimal anxiety (1990, 21). Thus, in the realm of information programming we can already find a microcosm of the disjunctural model of media flow in which constant adjustments and alternatives are made to fit specific local needs and interests.

Nowhere has this proven more important than in the distribution of evening news programs across the country. In the spring of 2000, faced with another round of budget cutbacks, the CBC made the highly controversial decision to abandon local news programs and centralize operations in Toronto. The 6:00 p.m. news hour, which had previously been produced by local CBC affiliates, would now be centrally produced and shipped out to affiliates across the country. The late evening news show, *The National*, would also continue without any corresponding local production. The outcry reverberated across the country, especially in the smaller markets and more remote, rural areas that felt that the public broadcaster was once again turning its back on its responsibility to serve the entire country and was now enforcing a centrist, urban perspective. CBC president Robert Rabinovitch was singled out for criticism and accusations of destroying the national broadcaster and, with it, the nation itself. Some went so far as to suggest that the only reason he got the job, in February 2000, was because he promised not to fight for the CBC and try to secure more money from Parliament ("CBC dead" 2000). Furthermore, his controversial statement to the Standing Committee on Heritage that it is sometimes necessary to "risk a limb in order to save a body" was hotly criticized as evidence that he didn't appreciate the value of the CBC at all. As Lise Lareau, president of the Canadian Media Guild said in retort, "The regional network is the root of the CBC. It's not just a limb" (Cheadle 2000). Of course, what very few wanted to admit was that this regional network was hemorrhaging anyway. Ratings for local newscasts on the CBC were dismal everywhere but in Atlantic Canada. Meanwhile, private broadcasters like CTV and Global did have success with their local suppertime news. This says something about CBC's inability to truly contend with local issues and speak directly to smaller communities while still maintaining a commitment to a nationalist ideal. Further, Rabinovitch's proposal was not to kill news altogether, but to replace local broadcasts with a national one in which fewer resources could go into a concentrated project. However, this was simply seen as another example of Toronto-centric, elite mastery over the airwaves that excluded the voice of the "every Canadian."

Surprisingly, even though the cuts to local news were spurred by major slashes to the CBC budget, Liberal politicians jumped onto the bandwagon and demanded that Rabinovitch back down from his decision. They did not, however, make any effort at all to consider reinstating the CBC budget, which had been slashed by nearly $400 million since the 1980s. The CBC president was very publicly called on the carpet during parliamentary hearings into the controversy. After various wheelings and dealings, both behind and in front of the cameras, a compromise was reached. Local newscasts would not be cut altogether but trimmed to a half-hour supplement to a new, national broadcast called *Canada Now*, which would be very visibly not produced in Toronto, but rather in Vancouver. Late night newscasts would remain cancelled, replaced by a greater commitment to nationally based arts and current affairs programming packaged with multiple broadcasts of *The National*. "Maybe we were a bit overzealous," a chastened Rabinovitch confessed, although pundits noted that this compromise was an optical illusion, seeing as how it did nothing to address the budget crisis facing the CBC (McKay 2000). Nor, tellingly, did it confront the uncomfortable reality that viewers didn't actually watch CBC local newscasts before and it was not clear if they would now with this revamped format. The important issue, therefore, isn't so much what the CBC actually does for Canadians, but in maintaining appearances for what it is supposed to do. Clearly, the idea of the CBC is far more powerful than its reality.

CBC radio has long been able to balance national and local concerns by mixing programming throughout the day and producing national shows from across the country, not just in Toronto. Yet, with the small exception of *Canada Now*, for some reason that successful formula has been deemed too unwieldy or too expensive for the television network to follow suit. As a result, the CBC left itself open to justifiable criticism of what has been called its embedded Toronto-centrism. Certainly, it does seem like the concerns of Toronto play far more regularly as headline news than that of any other city or region. And, unlike the private broadcasters Global and CTV, CBC's nightly newscast is not followed by a locally produced show. Interestingly, it is only recently that Global even ventured into the national news, preferring to focus its resources on locally produced shows. This is likely because local news has traditionally been much more successful than national news, particularly during the supper hour. A glance at the spring 2004 compiled more regional market ratings shows that locally produced news far outpaces national broadcasts. For example, in the Okanagan-Kamloops area, four of the five top-rated shows are local news, and only one national broadcast, *Global National*, appears in the top twenty, at number ten (BBM Canada 2004).

The importance of the local in information programming was driven home when *CityPulse at 6*, the news show produced by City-TV in Toronto, beat out both *The National* and *CTV News* with Lloyd Robertson for best news program at the 2004 Gemini Awards. The station, which is owned by CHUM, has also gone as far as to create a twenty-four-hour news station dedicated almost exclusively to Toronto-based stories, rivalling both CBC's Newsworld and CTV's Newsnet. CBC's decision to eliminate regional newscasts seriously impacted the public broadcaster's reputation in informational programming. In fact, in 2004, at public hearings to debate renewing Rabinovich's contract, it was noted that his decision to cancel local news resulted in the loss of approximately 200,000 viewers to private broadcasters (Cobb 2004). It is fair to say that local news is a major factor in how Canadians choose to receive their television and has even mitigated the penetration of satellite services that have fewer local stations available for subscription. It is also fair to say that the CBC has never been able to clearly articulate a local vision for its network and as a result fails to resonate on anything other than an ideological level.

The demand for local information programming is just as pronounced when it comes to sports. Viewer affinities with sports teams run extremely high, and public participation in the success of a team motivates high degrees of viewer attention. The extended playoff run of the Calgary Flames in the 2004 NHL playoffs, for example, demonstrates how a city can become fixated on the success of a local team as ratings skyrocketed and national news agencies turned their cameras to the celebrations on the city's streets. Further, sports programming is one of the few areas in Canadian television where geographic specificity is genuinely respected. In the NHL playoffs, for example, the CBC and TSN tailor broadcasts to specific markets and when games featuring Canadian teams overlap, the national broadcast is split. While this can be a tremendous problem for fans of the Montreal Canadiens living in the west, who, for example, were denied the overtime of a Montreal/Boston playoff game in April 2004 so that the opening minutes of the Vancouver/Calgary game might be shown, attempts to target specific games to specific audiences are used to minimize the common critique of Toronto-centrism levelled at national sports broadcasters, in particular the CBC, whose commentators are regularly accused of a bias towards the Toronto Maple Leafs.

The importance of televised sports to the Canadian broadcasting model, and in particular the National Hockey League, was stressed in the fall of 2004 when league owners locked out the players in a contract dispute. Unfortunately, for people like John Doyle who insist that hockey is the nationalist myth par excellence, the subsequent cancellation of the season exposed that myth to the ugly glare of reality. Despite all nostalgic references to hockey as integral to the national consciousness, interest in international, minor and women's league hockey did not receive a boost. While the three major cable sports networks, TSN, Sportsnet, and The Score, maneuvred to replace NHL broadcasts with AHL, world juniors, and European hockey broadcasts, the audience simply did not follow, causing one executive to lament, "The biggest myth in this country is that Canadians are dyed-in-the-wool hockey fans. That's a lie. They don't watch juniors. They don't attend junior games to a great degree. They don't watch the [American Hockey League], and you could say they don't watch NHL games involving U.S. teams. Just ask TSN about their numbers when the Leafs aren't playing" (Houston 2004a). The lack of audience for international hockey leagues, in which many NHL stars were now playing, demonstrated how resistant Canadians are to cultural change. Hockey was replaced on TSN with more basketball, lacrosse, and professional wrestling to anticipated lower ratings. The evening sports news shows also faced declining audiences on all three channels. The 10 p.m. news broadcast on Sportsnet, for example, saw its ratings fall from an average of 92,000 viewers in November 2003, to 40,000 during the lockout (Houston 2004a).

While a focus on the local team can be problematic for network programmers seeking to grow their audiences on a national scale, it highlights the fact that successful Canadian television is largely local information-based television. The CBC does well when it provides programming that is unavailable from foreign sources, such as hockey games featuring Canadian teams, and programming that appeals to specific local constituencies. Hockey fits that bill in a way unlike any other professional sport, not so much because it promotes a nationalist agenda but more because it is a part of local cultures. Similarly, regional Canadian sports like the CFL do particularly well in the prairie provinces where most of the teams are located. Curling, likewise, began as a regional, small-market sport played by semi-professionals who needed to hold regular fulltime jobs. However, since the Nagano

Winter Olympics in 1998, it has grown considerably on a national level.

Non-hockey sports broadcasting in Canada largely functions at a more niche level, rarely drawing audiences in the millions as the NHL playoffs routinely do. Major league baseball, for example, had no conventional broadcaster for World Series games in Canada from 1997 until 2003, when a deal was made with Craig Broadcasting to televise the games on the newly launched station, Toronto 1. Similarly, Craig Broadcasting acquired the rights to ABC's *Monday Night Football* when Global felt that they were not worth continuing, and the Toronto Raptors paid for time on Global Sunday afternoons, rather than being able to sell their rights. The problem comes from the enormous rights fees charged by the three largest American sports leagues, a situation that is financially imperilling even major American networks. Indeed, Fox lost $900 million on sports broadcasting in 2002 (Zelkovich 2004b). Rights fees for major league sports are increasingly prohibitive for conventional network broadcasters who are unable to offset the fees with advertising revenue in an era in which audience fragmentation has meant lower ratings and higher difficulty in creating "event" television around sports. This tendency has had the effect of driving televised sports towards cable networks, which can subsidize the rights fees with their subscriber revenue even before a single ad is sold. More importantly, it points to the way that broadcasters are being forced to rethink their relationship to their audience and envision different economies based on localized, fragmented, and targeted demographics. This new reality has interesting repercussions, especially for multicultural informational programming, as is evidenced in the surprising success of Fox Sports World Canada.

The limited success of Fox Sports World Canada, the only one of seven digital sports channels to be doing even mildly well financially, has been attributed to their practice of showing live European soccer games. The channel averaged 78,000 viewers for its coverage of the Euro 2004 soccer tournament, although its primetime average usually hovers around 3,000. It seems that Fox has tapped into a market that other broadcasters have consistently overlooked in their aim to build mass audiences based on homogenous notions of Canadian sports culture. The Portuguese-Canadian community, who watched the host team narrowly lose the Euro Cup to Greece, stressed the importance of being able to keep up with their local teams through grey market satellite at community centres and cafes. When the federal government threatened to clamp down on this exercise of multiculturalism in action through Bill C-2, which criminalized foreign satellite providers, the community publicly voiced their concern. The *Montreal Gazette* quoted Francisco Salvador, a Portuguese Canadian who regularly watched Portuguese soccer matches at a community centre in LaSalle: "If Bill C-2 closes that door, we would have to close. If we don't have the television, we have nothing" (Thompson 2004).

As Toronto Maple Leaf games migrate away from Sportsnet and TSN to specialty digital services like Leafs TV, it seems clear that local sports programming will drive the adoption of digital channels and broadcasters must be better attuned to the particular interests of their audience. The hope among cable and satellite operators is that local and niche sports programming will convince people to purchase bundles of digital channels rather than simply the narrower option of a single channel. Because the games are time sensitive, do not regularly appear in competing media such as the internet or DVD, and attract highly loyal viewers, they are a primary driver for television programmers who will increasingly strive to balance large-scale attractions like the Grey Cup game against more focused narrowcast attractions like Portuguese league soccer. The example of local programming, far from suggesting that television audiences are interested only in their own back yard, actually proves that globalization in the form of heterogenous media flows creates alternative forms of community that are no longer tied to a very narrow idea of territoriality but which provide a nexus around which immigrant and ethnic diaspora can circulate.

CONCLUSION

In addressing the way that a more global outlook on television programming can best respond to local needs, desires, and issues, the
term which may come to many people's minds is "glocalization." A
riff on the McLuhanist idea of the global village, glocalization refers
to the ways that global media, technology, and finance have collapsed
national and regional concerns to the point where they cease to be
relevant, leaving the local as the primary site in which globalization is experienced. However, we do not want to go that far because
it is clear not only in programming but also in the existing regulatory
frameworks for Canadian television that some version of the national
does still exist, perhaps nebulously, perhaps anxiously, but it is there
nonetheless. To us, this is a good thing, as the eradication of national
interests at this stage could lead toward the more homogenous form of
globalization that Appadurai warns about. As he states, the problem
of embedding global market forces into local production is that it exploits local labour, customs, and ideals in ways that conceal the real
sources of financial and technological flows. In that sense, then, local
production becomes little more than a fetish, offering the spectacle
of difference and specificity but actually engineered by mammoth
global interests who are orchestrating the identical process in loca-
tions around the globe (1990, 307). The *American Idol* juggernaut and
the way it took Canada by storm can be seen as one example of this
homogenizing form of globalization that succeeds through a fetishization of local interests.

Thus, instead of suggesting that Canadian television has become
an outdated concept that fails to resonate with citizens of this country,
it is more productive to consider how nationally oriented television
programming can in fact disrupt the rather surreptitious mechanisms
of glocalization. The key to unlocking the potential of Canadian television can be found in the prison walls of our obsession with American
programming. Certainly, at this point in history there is no way that
cable companies could simply remove CBS from Canadian airwaves,
or deny Canadians their weekly dose of *Desperate Housewives* – shown
with simultaneously substituted ads, of course. However, what if added

into the existing mix were more shows imported from other parts of the globe with closed caption subtitles, and other programming options that look over the cultural barricade that Canada seems to have built around itself? This is a risky proposition indeed, and one that requires creative cultural and business models by broadcasters and cable companies at national, regional, and local levels. The problem is, of course, that such a suggestion assumes smaller audience share, lower ratings overall, viewer fragmentation, and other problems which are driving advertising revenue and overall profits down. However, it cannot be denied that this process is happening anyway. Furthermore, the response of broadcasters to this problem hasn't been an opening up of the airwaves and a re-thinking of the potential of the disjunctured audience to build new markets, but a retrenchment into traditional models of broadcasting with the rather shrill insistence that the CRTC back them up in the name of national unity. Yet, a glance at Canadian Heritage's website shows clearly that the responsibility of the cultural regulatory agency is not merely to protect private industry from its own faltering business model but to build the conditions for a thriving national culture based on multiculturalism and openness to diversity. That is the promise of a future Canadian television, and it is one that is taking shape even without the support of industry and government. While there are still some who cling to the belief that the mediascape can still somehow be contained, advances in the technological flow of television have made it easier and easier to simply bypass the national broadcasting system with its carefully constructed schedule and transform not just what Canadians watch but when and how. The obsolescence of the network broadcasting model is not the stuff of the future but is increasingly a daily reality brought about by the combination of multiculturalism and new digital technologies.

CHAPTER THREE

TECHNOLOGY

Up to this point we have been exploring television mainly for the contribution that it makes to Canadian culture, but the history and development of Canadian broadcasting has also been inextricably linked to evolving technologies of telecommunications production, distribution, and reception. Various technologies have defined the way that we conceptualize television and the role that it plays in our lives, and in the life of the nation. To understand the dramatic scope of this technological transformation, recall that in 1949 there were only 3,600 television sets in Canadian homes, and no Canadian television stations broadcasting to them (Vipond 1989, 48). Today, Canada has more televisions than it has people, and viewers who subscribe to extended cable or satellite systems have access to channels that number in the hundreds. In moving between these moments in time, broadcasters, regulators, and citizens have negotiated a series of broad changes – the creation of the CBC as a national public broadcasting network, the development of CTV as a second network and second channel in the homes of many Canadians, the conversion to colour televisions, the introduction of cable television in the 1970s and pay television in the 1980s, the birth of satellite broadcasting, and the creation of a broad tier of digital channels, to name but a few. Each of these technological shifts changed the face of Canadian broadcasting as government and industry contended with shifting economic and cultural demands, which often appeared at odds with each other. Critics and scholars who have taken a narrowly technological look at broadcasting have often neglected the actual contexts and conditions for these developments. As a result, television has been conceptualized as something beyond the social, rather than as a medium that has been built in specific ways intended to re-shape Canadian culture and society. The point here is to move beyond the technological determinism that has long characterized the way television has been studied in this country, to consider television less as a "techno-cultural problem" and more as a "textual body" that is technologically mediated (Sconce 2004, 93).

In thinking about television as a technological form, our goal in this chapter is to return technology to the cultural arena. What we mean by this is that television has long functioned in this country in a schizophrenic state. On the one hand, television has been conceptualized as a bearer of culture, carrying a surfeit of images, narratives, and ideas about nation, community, identity, history, and territory. On the other hand, television has also been seen as a vastly sophisticated, ethereal network that transcends territorial boundaries and on which is carried huge capital ventures; therefore its ownership, investment, and control is very much at issue. These two ways of thinking about television are so far divided on a discursive level that even the federal government has chosen to split them apart, leaving Canadian television to serve two very different and at times oppositional masters. Bram Abramson and Marc Raboy detail a lengthy and convoluted series of governmental policy shifts in telecommunications during the mid-1990s that led to the closing of the Department of Communication, which had jurisdiction over all aspects of television. In its place, the newly formed Department of Canadian Heritage received control over television's cultural role: programming and production funding, the CRTC, the CBC. Its mandate is to foster the medium in ways that support Canada's official cultural policies of multiculturalism and bilingualism. Meanwhile, the actual telecommunication network is overseen by Industry Canada with the goal of fostering a knowledge-based economy and information society, to use two of the more popular buzzwords of the day (1999, 778).

The importance of this split to the development and future direction of Canadian television is at least twofold. In the first instance, television's role as a medium of culture has been hived off from the forces that actually build, control, and profit from it. That means that television is treated as a public forum, but one that primarily serves privatized corporate interests. This becomes increasingly obvious when the CRTC opts for protectionist measures like simultaneous substitution whose primary goal is the protection of a private industry, and which only provides trickle-down benefits to artists and audiences. At stake, then, is the consideration of television as a form of, or at least a conduit for, the public sphere. This idea, first conceptualized by Jürgen Habermas in his classic book *The Structural Transformation of the Public Sphere* (1991), can be briefly summarized as a social space in which perpetually ongoing public debate by private citizens can take place on the grounds of reason and logical disputation. Every individual is welcome to contribute, with the only criteria for involvement being that of having a well-thought-out argument. According to Habermas, the realm of communicative action is the lifeblood of any society, the place where ideas flourish and democracy becomes real. However, it has been mitigated by the development of private capital, the deadening realm in which money trumps ideas and discourse revolves around the consolidation of power, rather than the spread of democracy. This realm of money/power is not part of the public sphere but offers in its place a notion of representative publicity, of spectacle masquerading as discourse, and ritualistic consumption replacing productive communicative action (Calhoun 1994, 2–7).

For many, television fits within this category of representative publicity, an unconvincing replacement for a truly democratic, participatory society. Yet this disdain for the spectacle and the privileging of the literal, in which public talk is conceptualized as a good, while public display is not, can be seen as a flaw in Habermas's utopian vision. As scholars such as Nancy Fraser (1994) and Michael Warner (1994) have pointed out, this hierarchical formulation doubly marginalizes individuals who have already been placed outside the public sphere because of limits on their education, political, or economic rights, and who have historically sought access to public debates through the back doors of consumption. What is most interesting about this turn of events is the way that the visual and public display have in essence

challenged the idea of reason as a state of mind, separated from the
body (Warner 1994, 385). This means that rather than erasing mark-
ers of gender, racial, ethnic, linguistic, class, and cultural differences,
which Habermas's public sphere of discourse is supposed to do, a visu-
ally oriented public sphere has the potential to render the notion of
difference concrete, tangible, and very much a part of the lifeworld of
communicative action. In that sense, then, television continues to hold
out enormous promise within a framework of the public sphere con-
ceived not as holistic, uniform, and homogenous, but as replete with
a dazzling array of disjunctural bodies carrying with them an influx
of forms of cultural differences. It is our contention that the cultural
needs of television in a globalized environment of disjuncture and difference, to again borrow Appadurai's terms, have caused television
technologies to mutate from a single, mass broadcasting system to a
plethora of different forms, conduits, carriers, and networks that can
better serve its fractured audience. This polymorphous network is often at odds with the economic imperatives of the unified, all-encom-
passing telecommunications infrastructure as it is currently managed
by major corporate and governmental interests, and which has placed
business interests before the audience.

Another consequence of the separation of television culture and
television technology has been the fact that economic managers and
cultural managers often have very different agendas. As we have
demonstrated in the previous chapters, television's placement within
the Department of Heritage portfolio has rendered its cultural goals
inward-looking and nationalistic. Yet, the care of the infrastructure,
which is the responsibility of Industry Canada, has been far more
concerned with positioning Canadian television and telecommunications within an ever-expanding global market economy that is
technologically driven. In this sense, then, the division of television
culture from television technology is connected to concerns over the
so-called information society that is increasingly an economic, rather
than political, imperative. Abramson and Raboy make a convincing
case that Canada's telecommunication policy, as opposed to its television cultural policy, has been accelerating its global focus since the
1988 Free Trade Agreement with the United States. Furthermore, it has

done so based not on political arguments of "domestic necessity" but on economic ones of "commercial indispensability" (1999, 781). As a result of this imposed divorce between culture and technology, the "domestic necessity" argument has been taken over and reconfigured by cultural nationalists who insist first on a necessary and obvious link between political and cultural identity, and then use that as justification for greater regulatory protectionism with the argument that Canada's cultural survival is at stake (Collins 1990, 18). Nonetheless, the reality is that this is very much an inward-looking form of protection. The process is one that is concerned with protecting Canadians from themselves and their own debased tastes, and it has led to the sort of homogenous nationalism that limits the potential of television to mediate multiculturalism and helps generate a public sphere based on disjuncture and difference.

By contrast, telecommunication policies have increasingly undermined this kind of protectionism by integrating Canadian networks into a vast, global infrastructure in which capital flows freely, unmoored from domestic cultural or political concerns. The problem here is that separating television culture from television technology neglects to take into account genuinely important political concerns about identity and forms of difference. The commercialization of broadcasting, its value within the realm of money/power, means that the same kind of homogenizing tendencies that occur within national identity debates are likely to take place in the name of competition and constantly accelerating expansion, only on a global-economic instead of national-political scale. In other words, keeping culture and technology separate preserves a sense of defensive homogeneity for both projects while each provides justification for the other. Importantly, in both cases, they rely on a perceived threat of American cultural encroachment and domination. Yet, it was a technological decision made almost at the beginning of television that forever tied Canada's telecommunications infrastructure to that of the United States.

TELEVISION AND TELECOMMUNICATIONS

The long-term implications of technological change are not always apparent at the moment that important decisions about technologies are made, but it is clear that once they are made it is extremely difficult, if not impossible, to put the genie back in the bottle. Indeed, the most important decision about Canadian television appears natural and obvious in retrospect, but, had it been otherwise decided, would have dramatically transformed the history of Canadian television. Canada, like much of the Americas and Japan, broadcasts television according to the National Television Systems Committee (NTSC) standard. This standard, adopted by the American Federal Communications Commission (FCC) in 1941 to resolve the conflict that had arisen about a national analog television system in that country, differs from that used in Europe, Africa, and much of Asia. Because the system was utilized by the United States, whose entry into television broadcasting predated the first Canadian stations by several years, it seemed logical that Canada should use the system of its only neighbour. Nonetheless, had Canada adopted another system, such as the one used by Great Britain, for example, and barred the sale of NTSC-capable televisions to Canadians in the same way that efforts are now made to criminalize the reception of non-licensed foreign satellite signals, Canada could have shut the door on American broadcasters at the moment of television's inception. A decision such as this one would have meant that the Canadian television industry would have had the opportunity to develop along a completely different trajectory than it ultimately did.

Of course, had this been the case, it is just as likely that many Canadians living close to the American border, a majority of the population, and within signal range of American over-the-air analog broadcasters, would have chosen to circumvent the government by purchasing American televisions rather than Canadian ones. The grey market would have developed earlier in the history of Canadian broadcasting, and the end result may have been the same. It is impossible to know, since Canada entwined its broadcasting system with that of the United States from the time that the first stations were launched in 1952. The result of that decision is that important technological debates, such as those surrounding the introduction of cable and satellite systems, have revolved around the autonomy of the Canadian broadcasting system, and the perception that it is threatened by an American system into which we deliberately integrated ourselves, first out of a sense of domestic necessity (Canada has too few people over too much territory to effectively run its own system, better that it share); but now is most definitely argued on terms of commercial indispensability (viewer choice, technological expansion, free market competition). History appears to be repeating itself in discussions about the introduction of high definition television (HDTV) into Canada, in which the CRTC again chose to follow the lead of the FCC and American private broadcasters, rather than opt for a distinctly Canadian form of digital delivery.

At the same time, however, new technologies are redefining television viewing for millions of Canadians and undermining both political and cultural arguments for a protected national industry and an economic and technological infrastructure that is based on perpetually enlarged profits. Instead, these technologies are changing the parameters of the telecommunications infrastructure, opening up alternative markets and creating new audiences who are managing the flow of television for themselves, not just sitting back and letting the broadcasters do it for them. In that sense, they are responding to the ideological imperatives of the ethnoscape in which the constant flux of people, culture, and ideas necessitates new forms of media connectivity. Rather than a passive, mass medium system, television has become an increasingly interactive process as audiences select not only what they'll watch, but when and how. Interestingly, the three most common of these user-based technologies, the DVD, the digital video recorder (DVR), and peer-to-peer file-sharing (P2P), have been little remarked upon by the CRTC, even though they effectively re-route the flow of television in ways that significantly undermine regulatory strategies of cultural protection. Ironically, much more than HDTV, these three technologies have the possibility of reshaping Canadian television because of the way that they call into question the long-standing tradition of advertising-supported broadcasting. Yet HDTV is the only one receiving the attention of the CRTC, mostly because of its links to the American broadcasting industry that has quickly adopted the technology. Even though it generally frames its decisions with regard to their impact on national identity, the CRTC has seemingly overlooked the more serious challenge to the traditional model of television that is now possible through technologies that bypass the regulated broadcasting system.

It is important to point out that what is really threatened by the rise of new television technologies is the traditional model of dramatic programming, rather than the model for information programming like news and sports. This has to do with the way that audiences watch television for different purposes. In the case of information programming, the immediacy of live coverage keeps it secured within a traditional broadcasting model. When ones misses watching *The National* on any particular evening, the likelihood of downloading the show rather than just turning to the CBC's news website, or buying a newspaper, or waiting to catch up on the news the next day, are not very high. However, when one misses the season finale of *Canadian Idol*, the possibility of accessing it on one of many freestanding P2P services would be very tempting. Yet, as was explored in the previous chapter, dramatic programming is the cornerstone of cultural nationalist arguments in favour of a protected national television sector that is structured around the deliberate imposition of limits on audience choice that will ensure a semi-captive market. However, if Canadians continue to access dramatic programming through means other than conventional broadcasting, then the traditional broadcasting model can be seen to be on its last legs, and it will be time to figure out how to replace it. Before deciding that this means a triumph of the economic model for television supported by a freewheeling technological infrastructure, it should be pointed out that very similar concerns about television technology finding its way into the hands of the consumer echo in the hallways of Industry Canada.

New technologies that make television programming available to viewers when they want it rather than when it is best suited for networks have the potential to dramatically restructure the television experience so that the one-way flow of broadcaster to audience is permanently disrupted and sent bouncing through the mediascape. The reason for this is that the one-way flow model is based almost exclusively on the idea of a captive audience who is sold television in return for selling itself back to advertisers. Advertising-based television is so central to the television experience in Canada that it is sometimes difficult to recall that other models could have been just as easily developed. Alternate models of television broadcasting include the public, advertising-free model (such as America's PBS or the original model of the UK's BBC); the subscription-based model (such as Movie Central, and other channels dedicated to showing uncut films); or a modified ad-based model in which commercials are shown only before and after programs (as is common in Europe). Each of these models brings a different dynamic to television viewing and, consequently, television production.

　　There are a number of advantages and disadvantages that apply to the normative ad-based broadcasting model used by CBC, CTV, Global, and the major American networks. The most obvious advantage involves cost. Once a television has been purchased, viewers, at least those in major urban centres, can receive a variety of television channels over the air, at no additional cost. This model has remained more or less in place since the days of analog reception, although it has been adapted into a subscriber service for cable and satellite providers. Still, the experience of television tends to be something that is practically free and always available, and national and local advertising interspersed throughout the show supports the programming on these channels. A second advantage lies in the fact that ad-based models of television require no public funding and, therefore, channel offerings are governed primarily through a market system. Theoretically, an infinite number of ad-supported television channels are possible, if the advertising pool is large enough to support them. Third, ad-based television, because it seeks the largest possible audiences, focuses primarily on the popular, rather than on an externally defined value system that privileges socially ameliorative broadcasting. Unpopular programs, or programs that do not develop large audiences, are often quickly taken off the air. The fact that this applies to many Canadian programs cannot be overlooked. Indeed, the range of television production is limited by a need to please advertisers, and explicitly uncommercial, or anti-commercial, programs rarely make it to air except on the partially publicly funded CBC. A solely advertising-driven model claims only that the public chooses and the networks provide what people want, or what they believe a large number of people will want. This is why cable and broadcasting companies routinely invoke the rhetoric of choice for their audience, not because they really care about what they want from television, but because they are the ultimate commodity being sold to the companies who pay them and therefore keep the privatized, capitalist system of broadcasting going. However, if new technologies ratchet up choice in ways that completely bypass the broadcasting infrastructure, then business starts to falter and everyone, cultural nationalists and free market venture capitalists alike, is left scrambling.

For viewers inundated with ever-increasing numbers of television advertisements, commercials are increasingly regarded as an unnecessary irritant. Now that government regulators have given Canadian broadcasters even more ad-time per hour than their American counterparts, this problem is likely to get even worse. The CRTC's Canadian content proposal from December 2004 recommended expanding the advertising allotment in order to subsidize Canadian program content. It even proposed allowing fifteen-second mini-commercials on community access stations, under the banner of "sponsorship." Yet this decision occurred at a time when viewers have far more technological options to eliminate advertising altogether. What is at stake are competing conceptions of the way that television should be experienced and whether broadcasting as a medium will continue to dominate economically and culturally over other information and entertainment technologies. For Canadian broadcasters, the key is to keep viewers watching their stations in order to sell more advertising and at higher prices, which will in turn drive profits. For these broadcasters, technologies that permit time-shifting and ad deletion are enormous threats. For viewers, on the other hand, the ability to watch a program when it is most convenient, and to save time by eliminating the superfluous and unwanted portions of a broadcast (the ads), is taking precedence over any expectations of loyalty to a channel or even the system as it currently exists. As the CRTC moves to boost the amount of advertising permitted in an hour from twelve to fourteen minutes, it is clear that new technologies have pushed the traditional broadcast model to the tipping point. Ultimately, a variety of new technologies offer the potential to radically restructure the television experience. The implications are not only for industry, however. At stake is television's role as a cultural medium that can be controlled to serve narrowly defined, homogenous nationalist interests.

Many cultural commentators have derided the fact that commercial television regularly sinks to the lowest common denominator in its quest to maximize ratings, and that much of what airs is crassly exploitative and diminishes civic discourse. This is the argument most often deployed in denying the possibility of television as a medium for communicative action, and proving that it is little more than cheap spectacle. It is, really, a typical elitist critique of low culture based on the presumption that popularity denotes poor quality, and discussions about the latest life lesson for Bubbles, the idiot savant of *Trailer Park Boys*, are simply not valuable or socially redeeming in any way. Yet, others would argue that this is precisely the level at which culture is created and a sense of shared discursive ground can be established. However, both sides of this argument are compromised by the technological explosion on television that has fragmented the audience far beyond traditional conceptions of the mass. This has led to concerns that TV can no longer serve a nation-building role of common cultural experience at either the middlebrow level of ennobling and edifying culture or the lowbrow level of mass entertainment. Thus, the desire for a tightly controlled, homogenous audience with limited choice serves both a cultural argument for elite nationalist programming and the economic argument for maintaining a captive, manageable audience for maximized profit. The telecommunications infrastructure has been, therefore, developed along strictly homogenous lines that keep the audience in check. However, the industrial goal for ever-accelerating expansion has at this juncture in history created the conditions for its own undoing and given the audience a new level of control not just over shows and programming, but even over the airwaves themselves.

THE DIGITAL VIDEO RECORDER

Although only recently available in the Canadian market, the digital video recorder (DVR), of which TiVo is the best-known model, has significantly recalibrated the relationship of Canadian viewers to television. TiVo fan sites on the internet are overrun by consumer testimonials of the type that insist "TiVo changed my life," and even the staid *New York Times* headlined an article "How Do I Love Thee, TiVo?," which featured proclamations about how TiVo allowed teenagers to develop better sleeping, exercise, and eating habits by becoming better time managers (Taub 2004). The primary attractions of the digital video recorder are the ability to set the machine to record shows in a more intuitive and user-friendly manner than is possible with VCRs, a large hard drive to store huge amounts of recorded programming indefinitely, features that allow the user to pause and replay live television, and the ability to efficiently fast forward through commercial interruptions. Refinements in DVR technologies have even enabled the machine to "recommend" programming to audiences by keying in on certain viewer tendencies and linking to similarly themed shows. All in all, the promise of the DVR is the ability to create a highly personalized flow of television that exists without reference to traditional concepts such as networks, primetime schedules, or advertising. The situation is fast becoming acute. In a *USA Today* article, it was reported that in households that own a DVR, primetime viewing has dropped by 50 per cent. In the case of the 18–44 demographic, the most highly prized by advertisers, more than 60 per cent of DVR owners polled no longer watch their favourite shows in real time (Oldenburg 2005).

Thus far, the technology has been adopted by only a small minority of households, with 3.5 million devices sold in the United States to 108 million possible households in 2004, and projections for that to rise to 33.5 million by 2008, which is still only about one third the number of households which own a VCR (Oldenburg 2005). Currently, Canada lags significantly behind the United States in adoption of DVR technologies, primarily because industry leaders TiVo and ReplayTV were not initially made available in Canada. It was only in 2004 that cable companies rolled out multi-functional DVR digital cable boxes, and satellite services quickly followed suit. The reasons for Canada's sluggish and half-hearted move into this market are unclear. Perhaps it is simply the usual complaint against an industry that has grown lazy over generations of protective regulations and an overall lack of entrepreneurialism. Or it is the middlebrow anxiety that dismisses television as consumerist drivel and assumes audiences would be loath to take a more activist role in how they watch, as if admitting that they hate to miss an episode of *Desperate Housewives* or they're too tired to stay up late and watch *The Daily Show* would expose them to derision.

No matter the reasons why DVR technology has been very slowly adopted in Canada, it cannot be denied that while VCRs always carried with them the possibility of time-shifting television programs and fast-forwarding through commercials, the ease of use of the DVR has alarmed broadcasters and troubled the traditional broadcast model. The centrality of advertising on contemporary television means that the primary, and in many cases only, revenue source for broadcasters is advertisements. If advertisers begin to feel that viewers have stopped watching ads altogether, the very basis of commercial television is threatened. This possibility was suggested by Jamie Kellner, chairman of Turner Broadcasting, when he told *CableWorld* magazine that viewers who don't watch commercials during television shows are "stealing" from the networks: "Your contract with the network when you get the show is you're going to watch the spots. Otherwise you couldn't get the show on an ad-supported basis. Any time you skip a commercial or push the button you're actually stealing the programming" (Kramer 2002). While some might dismiss this kind of alarmist comments as akin to Jack Valenti's suggestion that the VCR would topple the movie industry, it is clear that they represent a real concern on the part of broadcasters. In November 2004, the United States House of Representatives debated HR2391, the Intellectual Property Protection Act. This act, which would have made users of peer-to-peer file-sharing networks criminally liable for copyright infringement, included a provision that would have criminalized fast-forwarding through commercials in television programs and through the ads at the beginning of DVDs (Grebb 2004). Although these provisions were ultimately removed from the bill that was passed by the House, the very fact that the criminalization of a practice that has been widespread for more than twenty years and that would be virtually impossible to police without a gross invasion of privacy indicates how new technologies have the power to disturb existing understandings about the way that television works.

Ultimately, of course, the $60 billion per year advertising industry is hardly going to disappear simply because DVRs make ad-skipping easier. Indeed, TiVo itself, under pressure from networks, began inserting "billboard" ads that pop up on the screen as a viewer fast-forwards through commercials, replacing one form of advertising for another. Further, many shows have increasingly returned to an earlier model of advertising, incorporating ads directly into the content of popular shows. So, just as Bob Hope or Jack Benny once performed in the ads on their shows, contestants on *Survivor* now play for prizes of "cool, refreshing Mountain Dew," and *American Idol* has their performers participate in music videos that push advertisers' wares. The threat to advertisers, it seems, can be alleviated to a degree by their own willingness to adapt and innovate, which has often been the hallmark of the ad industry generally. As a result, there has been a softening of their stance against DVRs by the major American networks, at least. According to recent surveys, the use of DVRs is turning television viewers into discerning audiences for commercials by fast-forwarding and then rewinding back if an ad catches their eye (Gershberg 2005). The real threat posed by DVRs, therefore, is not to advertising brands, but to the branding of the networks altogether. The DVR increasingly promises to make the idea of the network, and its carefully crafted schedule, irrelevant. While networks have spent years and millions of dollars creating particular brand identities for themselves, the DVR makes those identities inconsequential. If a viewer wants to watch *Corner Gas*, it makes little difference what channel the show appears on or when, once the DVR has been instructed to record it whenever a new episode airs. The traditional notion of the flow of television, in which network programmers attempt to create an evening-long block of programming that will keep viewers from moving to another channel, with one show flowing into the next in a logical and progressive fashion, is the one that is most disrupted by the DVR. When television becomes a smorgasbord rather than a fixed menu, it becomes harder for networks to build a loyal and reliable audience that they can then sell to advertisers.

Networks have begun battling this tendency by using programming tricks to thwart users of DVRs. Thus, for example, in 2004 ABC routinely extended the ending of popular shows like *Lost* and *Desperate Housewives* slightly past the hour. This meant that any recording technology would miss the final moments of an episode unless owners manually override the system. The situation was so pronounced that TiVo sent notices to their users informing them of ABC's policy so that they could adjust accordingly. ABC's scheduling chief, Jeff Bader, was unapologetic: "It's not my job to make it easy for people to leave our network. Our whole goal is to get people to stay with us from 8 to 11" (Levin 2004). Bader's desire to hold viewers captive through punitive tactics is at odds with the usual claims of private broadcasters that their goal is to serve the audience through limited models of viewer choice. While non-standard start and end times might irritate some viewers into watching shows live, it is not likely to be a winning long-term strategy. Further, as the utility of the television network as a distinct entity decreases, an emphasis on individual shows will only increase. It is this issue that may have the greatest repercussions for Canadian television, which has traditionally faltered in creating any content that defines a nationalist ethos and has instead relied on the telecommunications system itself. It is, as Maurice Charland and Will Straw both argue, a decidedly technological model of nationalist broadcasting minus any "semantic and emotional glue" (Straw 2002, 106). This may leave the country more vulnerable than others to increasing technological changes because the highly advanced technological infrastructure has been a fact of Canadian cultural and economic life. When it comes to broadcasting, Canada has one of the most advanced systems in the world and has quickly adopted digital and satellite technology to expand that system even further. With so much of the nationalist myth bound to metaphors of technological connection across vast territory, from the railroad to the CBC, the anxiety produced when these technologies begin to shatter that sense of territory is difficult to assuage. The reliance on the technology to produce connections while content languishes appears unchanging. Canadian television shows still suffer from lack of exposure and the market is once again missing out on new forms of distribution that bypass the telecommunication infrastructure in favour of models that privilege recording technologies.

THE DVD PLAYER

An important shift in the technological landscape of contemporary television is the marketing of television shows, both old and new, directly to consumers as DVDs. The importance of this new market was highlighted in April 2004, when the final episode of *Friends* was released on DVD five days after it was first broadcast on NBC. The short lead between initial broadcast and commercial release suggests that the old model of network television, in which the show appears only once before semi-permanently disappearing into the ether and only to re-emerge in syndication at a time and place virtually unknown to the viewer, is rapidly drawing to a close. In 2003 and 2004, the drive to release television shows on DVD took on added significance for the economics of the television industry, as DVD sales of television programs increased significantly. Through the first nine months of 2004, 470 television shows were released on DVD, up from 440 through the same period the year prior, with multi-disc sets increasing by 77 per cent. These releases accounted for more than US$2 billion in sales, an increase of more than 33 per cent from 2003. Further, analysts for Merrill Lynch estimated a 30 per cent annual growth in the area of television DVDs through 2008, with sales reaching US$3.9 billion at that time (Snider 2004a). Because the cost of a television show's production has been financed by its initial run and subsequent rebroadcasts, DVD sales are close to pure profits for television studios. The discs are inexpensive to manufacture, giving studios as much as $8 to $30 profit on every season-length DVD set sold to consumers. Hit shows on DVD, such as Comedy Central's *Chappelle's Show*, which sold more than two million copies in 2004, generate tens of millions of dollars worth of revenue in the DVD format. They also, as in this example, serve to generate buzz among audiences who may have missed the show on its first release, and shore up its regular network success for following seasons. When even shows with limited or nostalgic appeal, such as *What's Happening!!* (ABC 1976–79) sell more than 100,000 copies (Snider 2004b), the incentives for studios to migrate television to DVD is clear.

The creation of the DVD-watching audience, as opposed to the broadcasting audience, has a number of major consequences for television already troubled by the DVR market. In essence, it takes the audience completely out of the existing technological infrastructure and its corresponding economic model for sustainability. As noted before, broadcasters are responding to the use of DVRs by surreptitiously slipping in advertising into the regular show, either through product placement or through the less smooth insertion of pop up advertisements in the middle of a show. These digitally originated graphics, or DOGs as they're called, have become a mainstay of networks like Global who use them to advertise pizza and other entirely nonsensical products in the midst of their most popular shows. It is a particularly obnoxious practice that says much about the industry's contempt for its audience and for the medium itself. No one would expect an ad to suddenly dance across the screen at the local Cineplex; such an invasion into the dramatic experience of watching a film would be considered tacky and utterly disrespectful to the artistic creation. However, television apparently has no such high standards in the eyes of those who make a living from it, and the ease with which broadcasters disrupt a show to shill on behalf of their advertisers says much about how television is seen as a content-irrelevant medium. DVD television packages, by contrast, have elevated the medium in very interesting and sophisticated ways, by taking programming out of a matrix of passive flow and treating shows the same way that prestige film or music would be. The presumption of the DVD market for television is that viewers actually see value – critical, cultural, or artistic – in the medium and are seeking a more visceral, immediate, and active experience than networks allow. It is also true that DVDs tend to have higher visual and sound quality, include many additional features not available on regular broadcast, and when, where, and how much to watch are all issues entirely at the discretion of the purchaser. All these features effectively take the cultural product of television out of the hands of the broadcasters and cable companies and put it into the hands of the audience.

Another consequence of the DVD market is the way that it makes television programming collectible in a manner that was largely absent in the past. While some popular or cult-like television shows, such as *Star Trek*, were previously available on home video in greatest hit collections, these were very much the exception rather than the norm. Given the aggressive manner in which American television studios have been mining their back catalogue, however, it is increasingly likely that popular and unpopular shows alike will become available to viewers. In the contemporary market, broadcasts that might have been ephemeral have been given new life. For example, the November 2003 *Heritage Classic* hockey game played by the Edmonton Oilers and the Montreal Canadiens outdoors at Commonwealth Stadium was quickly released by the NHL and Warner Home Video. The idea of releasing special event hockey games on DVD – the 2004 Olympic gold medal hockey games featuring the Canadian men's and women's teams as well as the legendary Canada-Russia series of 1972 have also been released – would have been inconceivable prior to the shift towards television on DVD. Thus, some television programs can be turned into major cultural events only after the initial broadcast. They are commemorated by being inserted into the economy as collectibles, rather than persisting merely as tightly controlled archival footage, or as a cultural memory of viewers. It is a unique new way of recycling what Will Straw has called "cultural waste," products which outlived their cultural usefulness but then find themselves circulating in new ways, most notably as collector items (2000, 176). In essence, the DVD revolution in television has displaced a longstanding model of consuming culture and replaced it with one that puts the onus on the consumer as an active, participatory member in a discursive lifeworld that had previously been dismissed as non-communicative, non-participatory, and merely representative of culture but not really culture itself.

The increasingly widespread availability of older television programming on DVD erodes one of the important functions of television in recirculating old material. The rerun has been a central part of the television schedule for decades, and many local channels fill non-primetime hours with reruns of popular sitcoms and dramas. With the rapid expansion of channels in the world of satellite and digital cable, entire channels have sprung up catering exclusively to fans of old television programs, and many smaller networks like Comedy Central or Teletoon rely on syndication to fill programming gaps cheaply. The ability of television to recycle its own past, and thereby survive with less original programming, may be curtailed by the DVD revolution. This has profound implications for the ways that networks manage their seasons. Usually, a major network show is scheduled to air twenty-two original episodes over a nine-month period from September to May. That means over three months of the schedule will have to be filled with reruns, special programs, and other filler material. Since the ratings system uses a "sweeps" method in which extensive data is only gathered during the months of November, February, May, and August, networks save up their best material for concentrated bursts and then original programming all but disappears for a long time, often shedding loyal audience along the way. A *New York Times* article from February 2004 highlighted decisions by American networks to downplay reruns in an effort to staunch audience erosion. The networks planned to combat the loss of audience by ending their reliance on the thirty-five-week September to May television season, and by developing increasing numbers of series intended to run for fewer than twenty-two episodes, like *The Apprentice* or *The Simple Life*, that could be shown in bursts of eight to thirteen weeks to maintain viewer momentum. Significantly, these short run shows are also more saleable on DVD as they are less expensive to produce than a series running twenty-two hours or more and have the potential to further erode, rather than bolster, the audience for network television.

Nonetheless, while it is clear that networks are losing viewers to DVD, there also exists a significant reciprocal effect between the two forms. This was best demonstrated in September 2002, when Fox Television took the then unusual step of offering the complete first season of 24 on DVD just two weeks before the second season was to debut. This strategy to attract a new audience for the critically acclaimed, but little-watched, show seems to have worked, and the ratings for the second season debut were higher than those for the first season (Snider 2004b). Similar efforts to bolster the fortunes of acclaimed but neglected shows followed, including Fox's *Arrested Development* and CTV's *Corner Gas* in the fall of 2004. An even stronger case is offered by *The Family Guy*, the animated show that originally aired on Fox from 1999 through 2002. After the show was cancelled, it became a hit on DVD, finding a large new audience. The show's subsequent success on Comedy Network in the United States and Teletoon in Canada, coupled with the DVD sales, convinced Fox to resume production of the show, which returned to Fox with new episodes in 2005, after a three-year absence. *The Family Guy*, therefore, became the first television show to be produced primarily for the DVD market, with new episodes airing as a form of loss leader for the eventual collections. It is highly possible that this could be the new model of television production in a very short period of time.

However, if DVDs do take the place of network broadcasts as the viewing model of choice, Canadian television is not particularly well situated to capitalize on the development. Canadian television remains woefully unavailable on DVD by the contemporary standards of the form. When the 2004 Gemini awards were announced, the big winner, *Human Cargo*, was not available on DVD, nor was the Best Drama winner, *Da Vinci's Inquest*. Interestingly, the exception to this was *Trailer Park Boys*, which had the first two seasons available in one set, adding to its cult success. Producers are becoming more attuned to the DVD market. 2005's Gemini winner, *Sex Traffic*, was released on DVD in Canada in January 2006, around the time of the awards show. CBC seems particularly slow to release DVDs. By 2004, popular programs such as *The Newsroom*, *Made in Canada*, and *Degrassi Junior High* had only their first seasons available, and at considerably higher prices than American dramatic series. Despite the fact that the DVD release of *Corner Gas* did well enough to help boost the ratings for the second season, CTV has not tried to capitalize on the nostalgia market. 2004 saw the first collections of old sketch comedy classics *SCTV* and *The Kids in the Hall*, but in the American editions of the show, rather than the Canadian, and again at prohibitively high prices. And Canadian television producers have been particularly slow to release classic shows from the vault, such as *The Beachcombers*. It is clear, therefore, that Canadian television producers have been dragging their feet over providing material to the public, as if there is a fear that if the content takes precedence over the infrastructure the entire system may collapse. At the same time, Canadians have adopted DVD technology at a rapid rate. In 2004, Statscan reported that more than half of all Canadian households owned a DVD player, up from one-third in 2003 (Moore 2004). With so little Canadian content available to serve this growing market and at competitive costs, it seems that once again the Canadian television industry is deliberately ceding ground to American companies.

The Canadian reluctance to enter into the DVD market fails to make sense particularly when the issue of multiculturalism and foreign-language television penetration is addressed. One problem for DVD aficionados has been that different countries, in an effort to maintain staggered release dates or to protect the possibility of overseas network sales, have established regional settings intended to make it impossible to play a DVD from one country in a region with a different code. However, as is so often the case, these encryption codes were quickly broken and inexpensive region-free DVD players are now readily available. Importantly, it was the immigrant Asian community who largely spearheaded the region-free DVD market in order to make Pacific Rim film and television easily available to diasporic audiences. Most Asian shopping centres across Canada now have a steady stream of consumers in their video stores. What is most interesting is how this underground market has attracted a non-Asian community who are just as likely to purchase a $6 copy of the latest Hong Kong action film as wait patiently for it to be released in cinemas. Other immigrant communities have followed suit, importing a wide range of film, dramatic, and variety programming from their home countries in order to compensate for the failures of the Canadian broadcasting system to properly serve its multicultural mandate.

Just as with grey market news and sports programming, pirated DVDs are the last resort of immigrant populations who are otherwise denied access to their own cultural programming. Unfortunately, in the face of mounting pressure from the United States to fall in line with its copyright laws, Canadian officials responded in May 2005 with a showy raid of a suburban Toronto mall catering to the Asian community. A *Toronto Star* article on the raid spoke exclusively with police and legal experts on the issue, asking none of the people involved with the buying and selling of these DVDs if there are reasons other than price that account for this widespread cultural practice (Prashad 2005). What is most noteworthy about the raid is the way that, as with Bill C-2 and the attempt to regulate the grey market satellite industry, Canadian police agencies have specifically targeted the choices of ethnic minorities in this country in an effort to criminalize access to non-hegemonic cultural choices. Increasingly, the expansion of online DVD shopping has meant that television from around the world is now literally a few clicks away, and out of the hands of legislators who want to police Canada's cultural borders, and the international DVD market is expanding the scope of television from a closely monitored national experience to a much more diverse global one. The success of the British cult show *The Office*, which aired in Canada on the low-penetration specialty digital service BBC Canada but took off as a best-selling DVD set, highlights the way that DVDs allow television shows to bypass traditional systems and reach diverse audiences.

At this point, DVD technology does not need to be seen as a direct threat to television because it is still an alternative form of revenue. As in the case of *Corner Gas* or *Trailer Park Boys*, two of a very small smattering of Canadian DVD television successes, they can actually augment or enhance audience for regular broadcasts of popular shows, in essence giving them a second or even third life which might serve the increasingly worldwide Canadian diaspora. In that sense, then, the cries to clamp down on foreign-market DVD circulation seem rather shortsighted and hollow, in that they fail to recognize how important television is to sustaining cultures which are increasingly in flux as they move erratically around the globe. It is in this sense that the consumer-oriented representative publicity of television does offer a back door to the Canadian public sphere for groups marginalized from the centre of national identity formation and relegated as multicultural. Its existence as spectacle also attracts audiences from outside the narrow confines of ethnic communities and, unlike foreign-language television stations, the DVD market has quickly learned that the inclusion of multiple-language subtitles will lead to larger audiences. Clearly, then, DVD has the potential to shift the medium of television as a controllable technology in which audiences are dependent on the decisions of broadcasters, regulators, and service providers and organized into discrete national, ethnic, and linguistic audiences.

PEER-TO-PEER NETWORK FILE-SHARING

Not only is the internet a growing resource for international DVD sales, it is also fast becoming a clearing house for digital video files. The increasing availability of television programming online is a prospect with far graver implications for broadcasters. Its ubiquity was driven home in the traditional press in October 2004, when comedian and talk-show host Jon Stewart appeared on CNN's debate show, *Crossfire*. Stewart launched into an unprecedented attack on the show and its hosts, referring to them as "hacks" whose program was harmful to American democracy. The episode aired on a Friday night, and instantly became a major topic of discussion on political and media-oriented blogs in the weeks before the American election. Four days later, the thirteen-minute clip of the show had been downloaded 670,000 times from iFilm.com, over 50,000 more than the average number of viewers who watch *Crossfire* on television (Hines 2004). In the weeks that followed, 2.3 million people downloaded the file from iFilm.com

(C. Thompson 2005). This number did not account for the people who downloaded the file from other websites or received it from friends through e-mail. Further, the explosion of interest in the clip highlighted a distinction between old and new media. Significantly, about the only place where you couldn't download a copy of the file was on CNN.com, which instead offered to sell a videotape of the program to viewers, delivered by mail in the next week. Commenting on this disparity, Jeff Jarvis of Advance.net wrote, "Welcome to the future of TV! In old TV, a moment like this came, and if you missed it, you missed it. Tough luck. In new TV, you don't need to worry about watching it live – live is so yesterday – because thousands of peers will be keeping an eye out for you to let you know what you should watch, and they'll record it and distribute it" (in Hines 2004). Similar explosions of interest in such things as pop star Ashlee Simpson's lip-synching mishap on *Saturday Night Live* where she was caught mouthing lyrics to the wrong song, became flustered and walked off the stage, and the controversial Terrel Owens/Nicolette Sheridan *Monday Night Football* opening in which the *Desperate Housewives* star jumped naked into the arms of the Philadelphia Eagles wide receiver, emphasized the ability of viewers to catch up to moments from live television days or weeks after they occurred. These are not moments worth collecting for posterity, the way that an entire season of *Desperate Housewives* or the musical segments of *Saturday Night Live* are and have been released on DVD. However, they speak to the spontaneity of television and its ability to generate widespread public talk. With the advent of interactive websites, or blogs, these kinds of fleeting cultural moments that generate expansive public discussion are only likely to accelerate, bolstering the enthusiasm for downloadable television.

Networks are beginning to realize the power of the internet to increase the flow of programs to audiences who have neither the time nor inclination to stay glued to the set just in case something happens. ABC entered into a deal with iTunes to provide individual and season packages of their hit shows *Lost* and *Desperate Housewives* to subscribers at costs competitive with the price of DVDs. And network websites are offering clips of popular shows, although not always particularly well. When *Saturday Night Live* aired the popular gangsta rap parody

"Lazy Sunday," those who missed it on television rushed to download it from YouTube.com. NBC responded with threats to sue any website that hosted it and insisted viewers go to NBC's homepage if they wanted to see it. Unfortunately, in their efforts to capture this new audience through legal compulsion, they came across as out of touch with the new digital reality and, arguably, did more harm than good to *SNL* as an "edgy" brand.

In many ways, the changes wrought by both DVR and DVD have led to downloadable television. The digital format that makes both these technologies possible is a far cry from the rather bulky and difficult to manage analog recording technologies on which television was founded. Even when digitization began, the size of the files was far too big to be properly stored on temporary or disposable systems like ZIP drives or CD-ROMs. Thus, up until now, P2P has been largely an issue for the recording industry trying to stop music downloading through services like Napster. Now, with recordable DVD systems incorporated into computers and DVR set boxes, and hard drive capacity spiralling into the gigabytes, that problem has been all too efficiently dispatched. Further development in Blueray technology, which will drive the capacity of DVDs up exponentially, is just around the corner, as are faster online connection times and burning speeds. Sites like iFilm, which are largely subscriber based, compete with free P2P systems like Bitorrent, SoulSeek and YouTube. As technology improves the quality and adaptability of television, video files will soon be as hard to control as audio, if they aren't already. Interestingly enough, however, it is still primarily the music industry that is driving the fight against digital downloading while the television industry still battles over the increasingly fallacious idea of simply closing the broadcasting system to outside influences.

The Recording Industry Association of America (RIAA) lobbied successfully to have file-sharing defined as theft of intellectual property, and a number of legal battles have ensued in an effort to restrict or eliminate the practice, most of which have been largely ineffective. Yet, despite public campaigns by noted popular music artists like Tom Cochrane and Blue Rodeo, Canada did not follow suit. In 2004, for example, a federal court ruled that P2P downloading was akin to photocopying or taping for private use and was therefore not a violation of copyright law (R. Thompson 2005), and the Supreme Court of Canada called for legislation that took into account users, access, and creativity and not just the financial rights of corporate owners. Such a stand at first set Canada apart from the rest of the industrialized world, in particular the United States, and bolstered its reputation as a forward-looking country not afraid of technology. Not surprisingly, this has changed dramatically. Under mounting pressure from media and entertainment conglomerates and in the wake of increased criticism from the United States, a report from the Standing Committee on Heritage recommended drastic revision of copyright laws that would effectively transform the internet from an open source, user-oriented medium to a commercialized delivery system under the control of private corporations. Tabled in May 2004, *The Interim Report on Copyright Reform* was hotly criticized for an almost total lack of consideration for creative use and public access. Among its most controversial proposals was that educational institutions be required to pay a licensing fee just to have web access available in the classroom, even if the material being viewed was freely available. Some opposed to these recommendations, such as Michael Geist, a distinguished scholar and activist for intellectual property rights reform, noted in the media that the committee, chaired by Sarmite Bulte, had stacked their witness list primarily with rights holder groups and refused to find a balanced approach between this group and end users like educational institutions, digital artists, and the like (Geist 2004). The debate was renewed in 2005, following increased criminal action against downloaders in the United States and the announcement that Canada will remain on that country's watch list for copyright violations – a warning that is largely credited with having spurred the raid on the Pacific Mall in Markham, Ontario, to find pirated DVDs. Both the RIAA and the Motion Picture Association of America announced that they would seek to bring criminal charges against college students suspected of downloading sound and video files through P2P services (Bridis 2005). At the same time, the Canadian government announced that it would take the Bulte recommendations into consideration in drafting new legislation that would bring Canada back in line with international, U.S.-led treaties like the provisions established by the World Intellectual Property Organization in 1996 ("Government of Canada announces" 2005).

The threat of file-sharing is the possibility that it will seriously impact not only an advertiser-captive audience but also the value of television back catalogues even in their prestige DVD packaging. Further, like DVRs, peer-to-peer networks make the idea of television networks irrelevant. In an era in which television viewers no longer need cable, or even a television, to watch popular shows that can be found and downloaded from the internet, the concept of passive network flow is rendered irrelevant in favour of the flux of active audiences. The utopian promise of the internet is the possibility of making all television programming available to everyone, simultaneously, anywhere in the world. Canadians waiting for the CRTC to license RAI International or Aljazeera, or for TSN to start showing Portuguese league soccer, can theoretically bypass television altogether and access programs through file-sharing for free. There is also the possibility that international broadcasters who are tired of Canadian policies that try to keep them out of the country can start to provide downloading or even video-streaming services themselves at a regular subscription rate equal or even lower to that which cable or satellite companies would charge. This has already begun with services like JumpTV.com. At present, JumpTV.com streams live broadcast signals to subscribers from twenty-nine television channels around the world. The heterogeneity of JumpTV's offerings is astounding: Aljazeera (Qatar), Ceylon TV (Sri Lanka), Kanal D (Turkey), Inter+ (Ukraine), Telesport (Albania), VTV4 (Vietnam), and TV2M (Morocco), among dozens of others. The access to minority-language cultures available through JumpTV puts the offerings authorized by the CRTC to shame, and promises to place the internet in the forefront of the creation of multicultural connections and affinities. Each of JumpTV's channels can be subscribed to individually, with viewers choosing and paying for exactly the services that they want, and only the services that they want.

JumpTV enables the choices of television viewers, while the CRTC still seeks to restrict them. Furthermore, unlike cable companies' rather backhanded version of "choice," JumpTV's success stems from the fact that they view television as if the audience is important, while traditional stakeholders do not. Faced with overwhelming public demand for certain channels – whether American or foreign-language – the CRTC frequently decides that the public has no right to decide what it would like to watch. Streaming video television and file-sharing both have major repercussions for regulatory agencies like the CRTC. In a future in which viewers access television according to their own interests and schedules, the ability of the CRTC to keep foreign programming out of Canada will face serious challenges. With DVD and DVRs, the way that audiences have traditionally watched television came under threat. With P2P, the very idea of television as a distinct medium is now being contested through global technological convergence and grassroots innovations in non-capitalist exchange systems.

HIGH DEFINITION TELEVISION: THE TECHNOLOGICAL MCGUFFIN

In a case reminiscent of fiddling while Rome burns, the broadcasting industry has pinned almost all its technological hopes on high definition television to revitalize the market. Retail analysts anticipated huge sales of high definition television (HDTV) capable sets during the Christmas 2004 sales period, and commentators hoped that this might finally spur the widespread adoption of the technology in Canada. Heralded by industry, media, and government alike as the most significant change in television technology since the conversion from black-and-white to colour, HDTV has generated little consumer passion relative to technologies like DVDs, DVRs, and P2P. While there is no question that when all variables are in place, picture and sound quality is vastly improved, to say that it is as huge a change as colour was in the 1960s smacks of industry hyperbole. This difference is most noticeable and appreciated for highly detailed programs with a wide frame, like soccer, hockey, or football. The magnification of minute detail can, however, be a little scary for programs like the Academy Awards, where every wrinkle and mascara blotch is intensified. Furthermore, at this point, high definition offerings in Canada are relatively narrow and it is almost exclusively American networks that are providing the content. At the end of 2004, approximately 1.2 million HD-compatible televisions were in Canada, but only 180,000 of those were actually used to receive high definition broadcast signals (Blackwell 2004). By way of contrast, the United States had more than 1,100 stations broadcasting in high-definition one year earlier, while Canada only had three (Ray 2003). By mid-2006, Shaw Cable systems, which largely monopolizes the western half of the country, offered only nine channels in high definition. CBC only came into the high definition market in time for the 2006 Winter Olympics in Turin. Interestingly, it marked a return to the old-fashioned model of national broadcasting in which the feed came exclusively from Toronto, meaning that in Calgary News at Six airs at 4:00, and lets people in the west know what is happening in Ontario. A handful of additional channels have entered into the HD spectrum, broadcasting a portion of their schedules in high definition, although not all cable systems make the material available to subscribers. These are the national broadcaster CTV, local Toronto station CITY-TV, the specialty sports channels TSN and Rogers SportsNet, Discovery Channel Canada, the Movie Network, and its western regional counterpart Movie Central. In addition, many, but not all, cable and satellite providers carry the four main American networks, FOX, NBC, ABC, and CBS, in high definition way up on the dial. Canada's reluctance to dive into the high definition waters has been flagged by both industry and regulators alike as a major issue that will drive the policy process in a way that other technologies simply have not. CRTC chair Charles Dalfen called the discrepancy between Canadian and American service a "concern" in December 2004 (Brent 2004) and raised the spectre of viewers decamping en masse to grey market satellite providers for the crisper sound and video quality.

Despite the CRTC's insistence that Canadian audiences are ready to pony up huge amounts of money to upgrade their television systems and take advantage of what is in the end a slightly noticeable improvement, there is little to suggest that HDTV poses as great a threat to Canadian television as any of the three other technologies addressed here. To migrate upward to HDTV quality requires not only the purchase of a new high-end television but also renting or buying a set-top box from a cable or satellite company and paying the increased subscriber costs for the channels. In the end, you still get *Desperate Housewives*, only Bree's nostrils will be seen to flare that much wider. If this is the case, then why is the CRTC so concerned? Their argument is the quality of the viewing experience, which is still undermined by annoying commercial breaks, station identifiers, and pop-up banners. Anyone looking for purity would be just as well served to wait for the DVD versions of the show, which are in high definition but without the ads. Not coincidentally, though, HDTV is almost exclusively an American-driven technology supported by the large American networks. The fact is that NTSC has always been a lower quality broadcast standard than foreign systems like PAL and SECAM, so for many HDTV isn't a major advancement in television but just a way for the North American market to finally catch up to the rest of the world. Meanwhile, the three other technologies discussed here look beyond the north-south axis to a greater sense of global flows and imagine whole other vistas of television content, not just the chance to get the same show in multiple formats. No one would argue that videostreaming on your computer screen offers the best quality picture, but if it's the only way to watch your Italian soap opera, it will probably suffice.

For those who do decide to adopt HDTV, the benefits will not be immediately clear and in some cases there will actually be a marked decline in visual quality. A *National Post* story in December 2004, for instance, notes that "the disappointment of early HD adopters has been heard loud and clear by providers such as cable giant Rogers Communications" (Brent 2004). Among the challenges involved in selling HDTV services to Canadians is the fact that the image quality on high definition broadcasts varies tremendously depending on whether a program has been recorded using high definition equipment, or transferred to high definition from film. Further, a large percentage of high definition programming is regular analog programming that has been upconverted, and which does not look as good as other high definition content. If anything, many viewers have found that analog programming on HDTV looks worse than on a traditional television, either because it has the wrong aspect ratio, requiring it to be stretched, condensed, or shown with black bars on the sides of the screen, or because the HDTV highlights the flaws in analog material. The prevalence of analog signals, which will continue for a considerable period as old analog material circulates in reruns, is the primary reason that HDTVs are returned to retailers, as people find that they prefer the visual look of older analog sets (Brockhouse 2004). In the end, the adoption of HDTV by Canadian consumers has been slowed not only by its lack of clear-cut superiority to the older standard, but also by the clear absence of any really new or innovative content or viewer experience that effectively expands television as a cultural medium. In this sense, then, HDTV can be seen as the exemplar of a homogenous model of television broadcasting where the industry is trying to dress up old programming in new clothes, fooling no one and attracting few new audiences. Once again, the question why the CRTC has made HDTV a priority can be found, then, south of the border.

The rapid expansion of the HDTV market in the United States, particularly in comparison to Canada, has been driven by the fact that considerably more programming is available to consumers, with a substantially greater number of stations broadcasting in the format. This difference stems from the fact that in the United States, the Federal Communications Commission (FCC) mandated in 1997 that broadcasters had to switch to HDTV signals by the end of 2006. Further, in 2002, the FCC ruled that all television sets sold in the United States had to be HDTV-ready by 2007 (Ahrens 2002). This type of regulation was a break from tradition for the FCC, which had generally adopted a laissez faire attitude to new broadcast technologies. The CRTC, on the other hand, which generally acts to regulate broadcasting according to what it determines to be the national interest, took the traditionally American approach. In its ruling on digital television in June 2002, the CRTC opted to allow the market to drive the adoption of HDTV in Canada, refusing to push broadcasters to adopt the potentially expensive new technology. This decision, which served to spare broadcasters a costly transition that might not be warranted by consumer demand, has created the growing "technological gap between television services in

Canada and the U.S." that Charles Dalfen decried at the end of 2004 (Brent 2004). While Canada's intention, according to Michael McEwen of the HDTV transition organization Canadian Digital Television, "was always to lag behind the U.S. by a couple of years" (in Blackwell 2004), within two years of the decision it appeared that the risk was that Canada was falling badly behind on the technological front. It suggests one of two things. Either Canada has to quickly shape up to resume its traditional ten paces behind the American television industry; or, potentially, it could seek more equitable relationships elsewhere to balance off the economies of scale facing a country with wide regional and geographic diversity, large clusters of immigrant populations, and a comparably small population given its size. It is worth noting at this juncture that HDTV and digital television in general was also adopted with great fanfare by the countries of the EU, in keeping with the Television Without Frontiers mandate, to disappointing sales and lacklustre returns in indigenous programming (Iosifidis 2005, 63). It is not entirely clear why Canada, and the CRTC in particular, believed that it would solve their problems as a secondary world market for television.

The stumbling block for HDTV in Canada has been the costs associated with the conversion. During the 2004 Stanley Cup playoffs, *The Globe and Mail* reported that, despite strong ratings for hockey, the CBC had no plans to broadcast any games in the playoffs in high definition. The reason was that the approximate cost, $100,000 for a high definition production compared to $50,000 for an analog one, was not justified by the small number of Canadian households with access to the technology (Houston 2004b). Further, the CBC itself owned no HDTV-capable production trucks, although they were building one, and would have to rent one in order to produce the broadcast. For broadcasters, there is little short-term benefit to converting to HDTV, especially since audience demand in no way suggests that ratings will suddenly spike up and a whole new set of hockey fans will tune in to see with greater clarity if Mario Lemieux' skate really was over the line. Simply put, production costs will clearly increase, but revenues will not necessarily rise. This doesn't even take into consideration the massive start-up costs to convert the technological infrastructure to high definition, a cost that would most certainly be present in the minds of CBC executives who have to go begging hat in hand to politicians on a yearly basis. Given that the shift to HDTV does not generate revenue or boost profit margins, or excite audiences, the only incentive for broadcasters to make the transition is competition – or, more like cooperation or even collusion – with the United States.

In August 2003, CTV President Rick Brace warned about the capacity that was required to accommodate high definition broadcast signals, once again returning to a media scarcity argument that many thought was long over. He suggests, "there will, at some point, be no room in the tent. Generally, in the industry, you're going to hear rumblings about people getting anxious to launch HDTV. If you don't, you may find yourself before the CRTC asking it to take U.S. services off the grid in order to make room for Canadian [HDTV] content. That's going to be an issue because people very quickly get used to what they're receiving" (in Houston 2003). More than a year later, CHUM's Peter Miller warned that Canadian television was facing a competitiveness problem "if we don't go to HD and the U.S. [channels] go HD, we'll start to lose viewers to the U.S. services" (in Blackwell 2004). This is, of course, based on the assumption that Canadian networks will continue to air American programs using simultaneous substitution, only with poorer picture quality and more commercials. In which case, they may indeed have a point, but it's not one that will generate much sympathy from audiences. The possibility is that by adopting a passive stance in the face of dramatic American action, the Canadian broadcasting industry has placed itself at a competitive disadvantage with the only market they've ever engaged with, and continuing to insist it's the only market that matters. Yet, the fact that audiences themselves are not clamouring for the technology says something about how shortsighted and narrow-minded this view really is. Once again, just as Canada adopted the American broadcast standard in 1952, thereby tying the industry inextricably to our better-established neighbours to the south, the CRTC's HDTV policy, and the reluctance of many Canadian broadcasters to invest in the technology, has reaffirmed the centrality of American broadcasting in the Canadian context and denied even the possibility of a more global, multicultural perspective.

CONCLUSION

It is telling that in the case of HDTV, Canadian broadcasters are relying on old arguments about media scarcity and an American invasion that will crowd out national television until Canada is nothing more than a warehouse for foreign product. However, at the same time, they also claim contradictorily that the reason for HDTV is to better meet the demands of American programming in this country. It seems rather perplexing that they feel they can have it both ways: HDTV is necessary to both keep out and keep in American television. The overriding interest in this one new form of technology comes with little to no consideration of expanded audiences, innovative programming, or creative content. Yet technologies that do provide these kinds of advancements do exist and are being adopted at a far faster rate than HDTV. DVR, DVD, and P2P are welcome not only for their flexibility and ease of use, putting control over television in the hands of the viewer, but also, particularly in the case of the latter two, because they open up the airwaves to whole new cultural vistas. These technologies have the potential not only to dramatically recalibrate the flow of television, but to do so on a global scale that privileges heterogeneity and fosters dynamic audience interaction not only between the technology and the viewer, but between audiences themselves who have been kept separate by nationalist, ethnic, linguistic, and cultural arguments that appear more and more dated. If the purpose of the public sphere is to provide venues for open discussion and debate, for the free exchange of ideas, expressions, stories, and images, then the audience-driven technologies that are transforming television have enormous potential to erase the historic attitude against the medium as little more than a passive, consumerist spectacle. It, therefore, becomes politically urgent to question why Canadian television leaders in industry and government have refused to even consider moving beyond obsession with American competition to think not only more globally in terms of cultural flow, but also more locally in terms of audience participation. By remaining fixated on technologies that reinforce rather than transform the way television is used, Canada is once again missing a crucial opportunity to truly live up to its goals of multiculturalism and create new, global ways of transforming television into a medium of communicative action.

CONCLUSION

When the CRTC considered adding Aljazeera to the list of optional broadcast channels available to Canadian cable and satellite companies, they received more than twice as many comments in favour of the move as those opposed to it. Nonetheless, the regulator made an unusual decision about Aljazeera that they had to know would effectively remove the channel from Canadian airwaves, while at the same time gesturing hollowly at their own open-mindedness. This was a coldly calculated, some would say blatantly racist, decision, which manipulated a rhetoric of multiculturalism in order to undermine the aspirations of Canada's Arabic population. By way of contrast, the CRTC humbly backed down from its ruling against RAI International, after receiving thousands of complaints – including from Italian Canadian politicians. Some will point to the example of RAI International as evidence that the CRTC is willing to listen and adapt to the changing realities of Canadian society. However, we see it as really two sides of the same coin. RAI was ultimately incorporated into the Canadian television spectrum because it was politically inoffensive, while Aljazeera remained politically fraught. The only criticism of RAI was that it would interfere with the profit margin of a major Canadian media conglomerate, Corus. In this sense, then, the change of heart over RAI International, in the context of an entrenched attitude of suspicion toward a news and current affairs channel from the Middle East, highlights the problematic way in which multiculturalism is mediated on television so that it remains banal, inoffensive, and non-threatening.

Taken together, the CRTC decisions against Aljazeera and in favour of RAI speak to the embedded paternalism of the CRTC, but also to its increasing irrelevance. While the CRTC still aims to control Canadian culture by curtailing access to the technology, Canadian audiences are finding innovative ways to bypass television's cultural, techno-logical, and regulatory framework in order to make the medium more responsive and meaningful to their lives. With an entire regulatory in-frastructure built to protect private Canadian broadcasting interests, many of whom are presumed to be uncompetitive in a free market set-ting, the CRTC is unable to conceptualize the audience as anything other than a problem to be regulated. Indeed, as Richard Collins has argued, "Such terms as 'consumer sovereignty' and 'audience satisfac-tion' rarely enter into Canadian broadcasting policy discourse" (1990, 81). That said, we do not subscribe to the model of consumer sover-eignty or choice propounded by the Conservative party and the cable industry, because it is based on a "majority rule" system that privileges massive media conglomerates, homogenous programming, and keeps power tightly in the hands of industry instead of audience. It is for these reasons that we still cling – somewhat romantically some might say – to a notion of the nation as a gatekeeper of culture. Normally, that image suggests a carefully guarded portal that is rarely opened. In our case, we envision it being kept wide open but regulating the concen-tration of flows to ensure that minority voices are heard and become increasingly louder and steadier. Thus, we state categorically here that it is time to place the audience at the centre, rather than the periphery, of broadcasting policy in Canada.

We believe that the Canadian television audience is not a problem to be solved, but a promise to be kept. As a nation dedicated to the principles inherent in multiculturalism, it is time for Canada to step up to the consequences of those principles by enabling social and cul-tural difference, rather than trying to regulate it out of existence. This means opening up Canadian television to genuine programming dif-ference and embracing new technologies that will support a fractured, fragmented vision of culture. Television, arguably the most significant mass medium of the previous century, could well prove to be an impor-tant harbinger of a postmodern mediascape in which heterogeneity, disjuncture, and difference flow. Unlike the internet, which still has marginal penetration compared to broadcasting, or film, where the viewing practices of its audience have left it a poor cousin in the convergence market, television has a unique combination of regulatory, cultural, and technological features that suggests it rightly belongs at the centre of the media convergence. Indeed, the transformations of satellite and computer technology are already bringing the internet and film together on the home television screen. The film industry has begun to notice that for a large portion of the audience watching a film is no different than watching television. Evidence of this fact mounts as audiences fail to materialize in the theatres, opting to watch at home on DVD, specialty movie channels, or through digital connections to peer-to-peer networks. Already, industry leaders such as Wayne Clarkson, the head of Telefilm, and Viviane Reding, the European Union's commissioner for media, are discussing alternate distribution systems that will give smaller market films a chance on the global stage. In a presentation to the Standing Committee on Canadian Heritage's hearings on the film industry, Clarkson argued that Canadian film needs to stop measuring success against Hollywood box office and start looking for new opportunities, especially in specialty television and digital services ("Seek success" 2005). This is a golden opportunity for cultural producers, cable industry, and broadcasters alike. Yet while other media look forward, the one with the most to gain and the most to lose if it doesn't take action, stares forlornly at an imagined past of captive, passive audiences and a benign, industry-friendly regulatory system that invokes the sentimental dream of a nation that keeps refusing to come into existence, no matter how hard it tries.

For generations, television has been a medium whose primary use in Canada has been the construction of a normative national sentiment rooted in white, western, masculinist traditions. *Hockey Night in Canada* is perhaps the clearest example of this, and the fact that Don Cherry, a hockey commentator known for his racist and sexist remarks, is the best-known public face of the national broadcaster is demonstrative of how little interest Canadian television mandarins have in multiculturalism generally. A new model of television, and a model that will allow Canada to thrive culturally, must be based on destabilizing this hegemony by integrating white, western traditions within multiculturalism, rather than vice versa. The dream of Canadian broadcasters seems to have been to restrict the choices offered to audiences. The ideal for private broadcasters is large, captive audiences with no competition from within or from abroad. At the same time, however, Canadian audiences have long understood television through a sense of lack. Canada is the country where HBO and The Disney Channel are unavailable. Canada is the country where RAI International was unavailable. Canadian television is something that has been defined as much by its absences as by its presences, and Canadian viewers have long clamoured for more channels, more choices, more programming. This demand has been met in a limited fashion. Niche channels such as The Golf Channel or The Food Network have served to help fragment the audience across an array of hobbies and interests. Yet demands from multicultural audiences to further splinter the broadcasting model along linguistic and cultural lines are opposed by the CRTC, which clings to a protectionist broadcasting model, allowing only incremental change while attempting to shore up faltering Canadian broadcasting companies.

Increasingly, technological changes and growing frustration from the audience are transforming the playing field, leaving the traditional players scrambling with a weak defence. It is a system badly in need of fixing, increasingly at odds with its own stated agendas – both culturally to enhance tolerance, diversity, and openness to other cultures, and economically through the drive toward globalization and international markets. Yet, more than any other medium, television has a tight hold on nostalgia for Canadian national identity and cultural sovereignty as a dream perpetually deferred. It is time to acknowledge that television's greatest achievements cannot be met through the coordination of a homogenized, mass audience but must be accomplished through its ability to mediate multiculturalism as a conduit for images, narratives, and languages from around the globe. We are not suggesting that this is an easy transition, nor that audiences will eagerly abandon American Idol for the Eurovision Song Contest. Yet, signs abound that Canadians are not as closed-minded as some may prefer to characterize them. The work of globalization is already taking place behind the scenes through international co-productions, as cultural producers become acutely aware that their programs need to attract international markets. Even in such banal examples as *The Amazing Race*, which ended the 2004/05 television season as the most popular program in Canada, there is the hint that audiences are drawn to shows that reveal heretofore unknown cultures, albeit in exoticized, "othered" ways. Ultimately, just as the cultural mavens of the past envisioned television as a way to inculcate citizens into a tightly defined version of Canadian identity, we are agreeing with them in a backhanded fashion. We concur that television is an important medium for the construction of identities and public cultures. The trick is to play to its strengths as a medium of multiplicity and multiculturalism, not homogeneity and hegemonic nationalism.

The new television technologies that we discussed in Chapter Three – the DVD, the DVR, and peer-to-peer network file-sharing – hold the possibility to radically transform the regulatory framework that we discussed in Chapter One. The end result is likely to be a complete reframing of Canadian television programming. Nonetheless, the CRTC has been slow to respond to these new technological innovations, allowing them to transform television largely in a regulatory vacuum. While lawsuits and appeals are endlessly being filed to stop these technologies from proliferating unchecked, particularly around the issue of copyright, it has yet to be acknowledged that these transformations have done more to decentralize television and open the medium up to a plurality of voices than any number of regulatory initiatives could have. Television is flowering internationally, and Canadians have the means to access the best television programming from around the globe, putting us on the cutting edge of a major media transformation. More importantly, all Canadians increasingly have access to television of their own choosing, and programming that speaks to their own interests and concerns.

The technological transformation in which we find ourselves carries with it a genuine possibility of redefining our national culture so that it accords with our stated national principles in practice, not merely in theory. For years, Canadian regulators have stymied the growth of a truly multicultural television industry in this country, always using the threat of American cultural imperialism as the excuse. For Canadian television, American cultural imperialism is the great lie. In protecting Canadians from American television, the CRTC has provided Canadian networks with crutches like simultaneous substitution, which have all but guaranteed the dominance that the regulator ostensibly has sought to minimize. It is time to wake up to the fact of this lie, and reorient the way that Canadians think about television serving the interests of the nation.

This will require several important changes. First, it is time to acknowledge that the status quo is failing Canadians. As far back as 1995, Elisabeth Ostiguy pointed out that the current regulatory framework "was not designed for the new digital and interactive world of communications. Rules that once made good sense are rapidly being overtaken by events. These include Canadian content quotas, access guidelines for new specialty services, protectionist measures like simultaneous substitution, whether and how discretionary cable services should be regulated, the limitations against telephone company involvement in video distribution, and many others" (1995). Sadly, the regulatory situation has changed little since in the intervening decade, and the problems identified by Ostiguy have only become more acute. One change that could have a dramatic impact on the creation of a healthy indigenous broadcast culture rooted in the local would be the elimination of simultaneous substitution policies. Canadian broadcasters succeed in those instances when they use their local knowledge to produce material that Canadians want to see, whether this is *Hockey Night in Canada* or the evening newscast. Canadian broadcasters have a competitive advantage rooted in their understanding of local conditions and local markets, and they should be encouraged to develop these advantages by removing the crippling crutch of simultaneous substitution.

Second, Canada should cast wide its doors and welcome in as much third-language broadcasting as possible, ideally with available French and English subtitles so that foreign-language programming can have the widest possible impact across Canada. We agree with Rebecca Goldfarb that "Globalization requires a further move away from Canada's protectionist impulses and a greater move toward the international outlook stated in the 1995 Foreign Policy Review," because, realistically, the inward-looking orientation of the current regulatory framework has utterly failed to create a national broadcasting system that accurately reflects this nation (1997, 43). Chinese films, Spanish novels, and even Japanese comic books are all widely available to Canadian cultural consumers, but television, that highly regulated medium, is increasingly the subject of a problematic foreign-language gap. That is unsupportable. Canada should be opening up its television industry to foreign-language broadcasters, not only because the internet and grey market satellites make it economically necessary, but because it is the right thing to do in a nation that claims to champion multiculturalism. Canadian broadcasters should be embracing niche programming for everyone, not simply for golfers and aspiring chefs.

If Canada is to do more than provide lip service to multiculturalism, it is necessary to rethink the relationship between the local, the national, and the global. It is incumbent on Canadian television producers to more actively engage in local programming, rather than attaching themselves to American exports that are already made available in this country by border stations. Canadian television networks cannot content themselves with being simple rebroadcasters of American content, or changing television technologies will make them irrelevant. This is not simply an argument about how Canadian television stations should proceed in an ideal world, but a recognition that the traditional broadcasting model is rapidly collapsing, and that without radical changes Canadian networks are in a poor position to deal with the change. At the same time, Canada must increase its embrace of the global cultural networks. Canada has long prided itself on the welcome that it offers immigrants from around the world, and the country should be justly proud of its efforts to integrate diasporic communities. At the same time, much more needs to be done. If Canadians are serious when they discuss the country as a mosaic rather than a melting pot, then legitimate and constructive efforts to open up the country to diverse cultures need to be made. Canada should throw its television culture open to the world in order to better serve the cultural needs of all of its citizens.

These changes – an increasing attention to the local coupled with a genuine welcoming of the global – would have the end result of helping to redefine the national culture of Canada in important and unpredictable ways. By placing the local and the global in a new dynamic relationship with each other, and by embracing difference, diversity, and plurality in more critical and socially grounded ways, the possibility emerges to create new understandings of our national culture that move beyond a reductionist relationship of Canada to the United States and England. Canada can no longer cling to definitions of nationalism rooted in nineteenth-century beliefs but must embrace doubt, difference, and diversity as the new models of nation-building. If Canadian television can be understood as AmericaPlus because of the way that it offers most of what is available south of us plus additional programming, then it is time to acknowledge that the possibility exists to turn Canadian television into GlobalPlus, by relegating American television to simply one option within an overall structure of multinational and multicultural offerings. As the central carrier of culture in this country, television is an important locus of social and cultural values. It is time that the country reshapes it to better reflect those values that have long been held to be the defining features of this nation.

WORKS CITED

Abramson, Bram Dov, and Marc Raboy. 1999. "Policy globalization and the 'information society': A View from Canada." *Telecommunications Policy* 23: 775–91.

Ahrens, Frank. 2002. "FCC moves to speed shift to digital TV." *Washington Post*, August 9, A01.

Allemang, John. 2004. "Does the CBC know what it's doing?" *Globe and Mail*, November 27, R1.

"A nice haul for Cargo." 2004. *Toronto Star*, December 14, D05.

Appadurai, Arjun. 1990. "Disjuncture and difference in the global cultural economy." In *Global Culture: Nationalism, Globalization and Modernity*, edited by Mike Featherstone. 295–310. London: Sage.

Atherton, Tony. 2004. "Human Cargo delivers plight of refugees." *Calgary Herald*, January 3, ES12.

Attallah, Paul, and Leslie Regan Shade, eds. 2002. *Mediascapes: New patterns in Canadian communication*. Scarborough, ON: Thomson Nelson.

Babe, Robert. 1990. *Telecommunications in Canada: Technology, industry, and government*. Toronto: University of Toronto Press.

BBM Canada. 2004. "TV data market tidbits" Spring. Available: http://www. bbm.ca/en/tv_tidbits.html

Beaty, Bart, and Rebecca Sullivan. 2003. "Canadian television: Industry, audience and technology." In *How Canadians communicate*, edited by David Taras, Frits Pannekoek, and Maria Bakardjieva, 143–64. Calgary: University of Calgary Press.

Blackwell, Richard. 2004. "HDTV's future getting in focus." *Globe and Mail*, December 6, B1.

Brent, Paul. 2004. "HDTV lacks programs." *National Post*, December 2, FP2.

Bridis, Ted. 2005. "Recording industry attacks file sharing on new research net." *Montreal Gazette*, April 13, B10.

Brockhouse, Gordon. 2004. "Glitches fail to dull growing appetite for HDTV." *Globe and Mail*, August 26, B10.

Calhoun, Craig. 1994. "Introduction: Habermas and the public sphere." In *Habermas and the public sphere*, edited by Craig Calhoun, 1–50. Cambridge, MA: MIT Press.

"Canada is lucky we allow them to exist." 2004. Available: http://www.tblog. com/templates/index.php?bid=sisterstalk&static=351941

"Canadian dramas axed as funding pared." 2004. *Calgary Herald*, February 20, D11.

Canadian Heritage. 2005. "Multiculturalism: What is multiculturalism?" Available: http://www.canadianheritage.gc.ca/progs/multi/what-multi_ e.cfm

"Canadian Idol salutes Canadian icon Gordon Lightfoot August 18 and 19 on CTV." 2004. CTV News Release. August 16.

Canadian Press. 2004. "Something old, something new in CBC schedule." May 27. Available: http://www.publicairwaves.ca/index.php?page=675

Canadian Television Fund. http://www.canadiantelevisionfund.ca. Accessed April 2005.

"Canadian TV an 'unholy mess,' Gross tells fellow actors." 2004. *Kitchener-Waterloo Record*, June 2.

"CBC dead without restored funding." 2000. *Toronto Star*, June 6, A23.

Charland, Maurice. 2004. "Technological nationalism." In *Communication history in Canada*, edited by Daniel J. Robinson, 28-39. Toronto: Oxford University Press.

Cheadle, Bruce. 2000. "Grits demand money for CBC local newscasts." CP Newswire, May 17.

Cobb, Chris. 2004. "CBC asks for an extra $100M to save regional programming," *Ottawa Citizen*, November 16, A4.

Colker, David. 2004. "Hey, you need a license to watch that!" *Los Angeles Times*, August 19, C1.

Collins, Richard. 1990. *Culture, communication, and national identity: The case of Canadian television*. Toronto: University of Toronto Press.

Collins, Richard. 2002. *Media and identity in contemporary Europe: Consequences of global convergence*. Bristol, UK: Intellect Books.

Community Media Education Society. 2001. Letter to the CRTC, January 30. Available: http://www.vcn.bc.ca/cmes/1pages/letrjan.htm

CRTC. "The CRTC's origins." Available: http://www.crtc.gc.ca/eng/BACKGRND/Brochures/B19903.htm

CRTC. 2004a. "Broadcasting public notice CRTC 2004–50." May 15. Available: http://www.crtc.gc.ca/eng/public/2004/8045/noticebr.htm

CRTC. 2004b. "Broadcasting public notice CRTC 2004–88." November 18. Available: http://www.crtc.gc.ca/eng/public/2004/8045/noticebr.htm

CRTC. 2006. "The CRTC releases its final report on financial results for private television in Canada." March 28. Available: http://www.crtc.gc.ca/eng/NEWS/RELEASES/2006/r060328.htm

Curry, Bill. 2006. "NDP alarmed at talk of easing telecom cap." *Globe and Mail,* March 28, B6.

Davidson, Sean. 2004. "Global uncertainty." *Playback Magazine,* November 22, 23.

Den Tandt, Michael. 2005. "Cross border amity eroding: Poll." *Globe and Mail,* May 9, A1.

Dixon, Guy. 2006. "CBC-TV names new head of arts." *Globe and Mail.* March 30. R1.

Dorland, Michael, ed. 1996. *The Cultural industries in Canada: Problems, policies, and prospects.* Toronto: James Lorimer.

Dorland, Michael, and Maurice Charland. 2002. *Law, rhetoric and irony in the formation of Canadian civil culture.* Toronto: University of Toronto Press.

Doyle, John. 2004. "It takes ice to make a real Canadian reality show." *Globe and Mail,* September 21, R2.

Druick, Zoë. 2006. "International cultural relations as a factor in postwar Canadian cultural policy: The relevance of UNESCO for the Massey Commission." *Canadian journal of communication* 31 (March): 177–95.

Fraser, Nancy. 1994. "Rethinking the public sphere: A contribution to the critique of actually existing democracy." *Habermas and the public sphere,* edited by Craig Calhoun, 109–42. Cambridge, MA: MIT Press.

Friends of Canadian Broadcasting. "Goals and priorities." 2005. Available: http://www.friends.ca/About_Us/priorities.asp

Friesen, Joe. 2004. "Harper's CBC views draw fire." *Globe and Mail,* May 20, A7.

Gasher, Mike. 1997. "From sacred cows to white elephants: Cultural policy under siege." In *Canadian cultures and globalization,* edited by Joy Cohnstaedt and Yves Frenette, 13–30. Montreal: Association for Canadian Studies.

Geist, Michael. 2004. "Copyright reform needs a balanced approach." *Toronto Star,* June 14, D5.

Gershberg, Michele. 2005. "TV networks say digital recorders raise viewership." *Yahoo News.* November 16. Available: http://news.yahoo.com/s/nm/20051116/tv_nm/media_television_dvr_dc

Gill, Alexandra. 2004. "Reality bites Canada." *Globe and Mail,* May 22, R1.

Goldfarb, Rebecca. 1997. "External constraints on public policy: Canada's struggle to preserve a broadcasting system fundamentally Canadian in character." In *Canadian cultures and globalization,* edited by Joy Cohnstaedt and Yves Frenette, 31–46. Montreal: Association for Canadian Studies.

"Government must support TV drama, Gross demands." 2004. *Globe and Mail,* June 2, R2.

"Government of Canada announces upcoming amendments to the copyright act." 2005. March 24. Available: http://www.ic.gc.ca/cmb/welcomeic.nsf/261ce500dfcd7259852564820068dc6d/85256a5d006b972085256fcd0078718c!OpenDocument

Grebb, Michael. 2004. "Senate may ram copyright bill." *Wired.* Available: http://www.wired.com/news/politics/0,1283,65704,00.html

Gripsrud, Jostein. 2004. "Broadcast television: The chances of its survival in a digital age." In *Television after TV: Essays on a medium in transition,* edited by Lynn Spigel and Jan Olsson, 210–23. Durham, NC: Duke University Press.

Habermas, Jürgen. 1991. *The structural transformation of the public sphere: An inquiry into a category of bourgeois society.* Cambridge, MA: MIT Press.

Higgins, John W. 1999. "Community television and the vision of media literacy, social action, and empowerment." *Journal of broadcasting and electronic media* 43.4 (Fall): 624–44.

Hines, Matt. 2004. "Jon Stewart 'Crossfire' feud ignites net frenzy." *CNET News.com.* October 19.

Hogarth, David. 2002. *Documentary television in Canada: From public service to global marketplace.* Montreal and Kingston: McGill-Queen's University Press.

Houston, William. 2003. "Here's what HDTV means to the viewers." *Globe and Mail,* August 22, S5.

Houston, William. 2004a. "CBC will have no truck with HDTV in playoffs." *Globe and Mail,* May 1.

Houston, William. 2004b. "Lockout batters networks' audiences." *Globe and Mail,* November 27, S1.

Hutcheon, Linda. 1988. *The Canadian postmodern: A study of contemporary English-Canadian fiction.* Toronto: Oxford University Press.

"Idol hopefuls get advice from Gordon Lightfoot." 2004. *CTV.ca*, August 18. Available: http://www.ctv.ca/servlet/ArticleNews/story/ CTVNews/1092830506541_281?hub=Entertainment

Iosifidis, Petros, Jeanette Steemers, and Mark Wheeler. 2005. *European television industries*. London: BFI Publishing.

Jack, Ian. 2004. "Tories would slash CRTC role." *National Post*, June 10, FP1.

King, Donna L. and Christopher Mele. 1999. "Making public access television: Community participation, media literacy, and the public sphere." *Journal of broadcasting and electronic media* 43.4 (Fall): 603–25.

Kohanik, Eric. 2005. "Another chance for Cargo." *Montreal Gazette*, January 11, D7.

Kramer, Staci D. 2002. "Content's king." *CableWorld*, April 29. Available: http:// www.broadband-pbimedia.com/cgi/cw/show_mag.cgi?pub=cw&mon=042 902&file=contents_king.inc

Lazarus, David. 2004. "Cable strangles choice." *San Francisco Chronicle*, May 16, J1.

Levin, Gary. 2004. "Shows start and end just off the half-hour." *USA Today*. Available: http://www.usatoday.com/life/television/news/2004-11-28-tv-schedule_x.htm

MacDonald, Gayle. 2004a. "Looking for the new Friends." *Globe and Mail*, May 18, R1.

MacDonald, Gayle. 2004b. "CBC films offer good defence." *Globe and Mail*, November 10, R3.

Mackey, Eva. 1999. *The House of difference: Cultural politics and national identity in Canada*. New York: Routledge.

Mah, Bill. 2004. "Cable won't run Arab news channel despite CRTC approval." *Edmonton Journal*, July 16, A3.

Manning, Erin. 2003. *Ephemeral territories: Representing nation, home, and identity in Canada*. Minneapolis: University of Minnesota Press.

McKay, John. 2000. "CBC cuts local newscasts in half." *Montreal Gazette*, May 30, F6.

McNamara, Lynne. 2004. "Human Cargo had genesis in refugee board hearings." *Vancouver Sun*, January 5, C6.

Moore, Oliver. 2004. "Canadians buy into digital age." *Globe and Mail Online*, December 13. Available: http://www.theglobeandmail.com/servlet/Page/ document/v4/sub/MarketingPage?user_URL=http://www.theglobeand-mail.com%2Fservlet%2Fstory%2FRTGAM.20041213.wstat1213%2FBNStory %2FNational%2F%3Fquery%3Dcanadians%2Bbuy%2Binto%2Bdigital&ord=

17638188&brand=theglobeandmail&redirect_reason=2&denial_reasons=13
53701%3A4%3B1171941%3A4%3B&force_login=false

Morley, David. 2000. *Home territories: Media, mobility and identity*. New York: Routledge.

Mulroney, Ben. 2004. "A walk to remember." *TV Guide*, April 3, 6.

Neihart, Ben. 2005. "... OMG! < > I Love Ellie and Ashley. < ... Craig Is Totally HOTTTT. < > DGrassi Is tha Best Teen TV N da WRLD! <." *New York Times Magazine*, March 20. 40–45.

"Networks up Canadian content." 2004. *The Record*, September 8. Available: http://www.friends.ca/News/Friends_News/archives/articles09080401. asp

"New shows finally falling into place." 2000. *Toronto Star*, September 19, F5.

Oldenburg, Ann. 2005. "TiVo's ripple effect: Water-cooler chill." *USA Today*, March 24, 1D.

Ostiguy, Elisabeth. 1995. "The benefits of more choice in distribution channels for cultural programming." *Canadian journal of communication* 20(3). Available: http://www.cjc-online.ca/viewarticle.php?id=304&layout=html

Posner, Michael. 2005. "TV producers blast fund's 'parochial' Canadian-content rules." *Globe and Mail*, February 14, R1.

Prashad, Sharda. 2005. "Pirated DVDs seized at mall." *Toronto Star*, May 5, B.04.

Quill, Greg. 2004. "Actors, writers make a play for neglected culture issues." *Toronto Star*, June 17, A8.

Raboy, Marc. 1990. *Missed opportunities: The story of Canada's broadcasting policy*. Montreal and Kingston: McGill-Queen's University Press.

Ray, Randy. 2003. "HDTV finally ready for prime time." *Globe and Mail*, November 17, F6.

Reguly, Eric. 2004. "Why is Harper bent on gutting the CRTC?" *Globe and Mail*, June 12, B2.

Robertson, Grant, and Catherine McLean. 2006a. "CRTC favours choice." *Globe and Mail*, February 26.

Robertson, Grant, and Catherine McLean. 2006b. "CRTC says go and pick your own TV channels." *Globe and Mail*, February 28. B1.

Sconce, Jeffrey. 2004. "What if?: Charting television's new textual boundaries." In *Television after TV: Essays on a Medium in Transition*, edited by Lynn Spigel and Jan Olsson, 93–112. Durham, NC: Duke University Press.

"Seek success beyond box office: Telefilm head." 2005. *CBC News Online*, March 11. Available: http://www.cbc.ca/story/arts/national/2005/03/11/Arts/ clarksontelefilm050311.html

"Signal substitution, protecting the Canadian broadcasting industry." 2004. CRTC News Release, January 30. Available: http://www.crtc.gc.ca/ENG/NEWS/RELEASES/2004/i040130.htm

Snider, Mike. 2004a. "Old TV shows never die...." *USA Today*, October 17. Available: http://www.usatoday.com/life/television/news/2004-10-17-tv-dvds-main_x.htm

Snider, Mike. 2004b. "TV shows rerun profitably on DVD." *USA Today*, October 17. Available: http://www.usatoday.com/life/television/news/2004-10-17-tv-dvds_x.htm

"Sports reality shows not making the cut." 2004. *Metronews*, October 8. Available: http://www.metronews.ca/sports_news_fullstory.asp?id=3792

Statistics Canada. 2005. "Television viewing: data tables." March, catalogue no. 87F0006XIE. Available: http://www.statcan.ca:80/english/freepub/87F0006XIE/2005001/sumtable2005001.htm

Straw, Will. 2000. "Exhausted commodities: The material culture of music." *Canadian journal of communication* 25(1). Available: http://www.cjc-online.ca/viewarticle.php?id=571

Straw, Will. 2002. "Dilemmas of definition." In *Slippery pastimes: Reading the popular in Canadian culture*, edited by Jeannette Sloniowski and Joan Nicks, 95–108. Waterloo: Wilfrid Laurier University Press.

Taras, David, Frits Pannekoek, and Maria Bakardjieva, eds. 2003. *How Canadians communicate*, Calgary: University of Calgary Press.

Taub, Eric A. 2004. "How do I love thee, TiVo?" *New York Times*, March 18. Available: http://tech2.nytimes.com/mem/technology/techreview.html?res=9D04E5DB1531F93BA25750C0A9629C8B63

Taylor, Charles. 1992. *Multiculturalism and "the politics of recognition,"* edited and introduced by Amy Gutmann with commentary by Steven C. Rockefeller, Michael Walzer, and Susan Wolf. Princeton: Princeton University Press.

Thompson, Clive. 2005. "The BitTorrent effect," *Wired*, January. Available: http://www.wired.com/wired/archive/13.01/bittorrent.html

Thompson, Elizabeth. 2004. "Satellite crackdown angers ethnic groups." *Montreal Gazette*, May 12, A14.

Thompson, Robert. 2005. "Music industry renews battle over file sharing." *Calgary Herald*, April 21, A3.

Tinic, Serra. 2005. *On location: Canada's television industry in a global market*. Toronto: University of Toronto Press.

"Tories would gut film, TV production, industry complains." 2004. *CBC Online*, June 11. Available: http://www.cbc.ca/stories/2004/06/11/canada/harper-culture040610

Tracey, M., and W. Redal. 1995. "The new parochialism: The triumph of the populist in the flow of international television." *Canadian journal of communication* 20(3). Available: http://www.cjc-online.ca/viewarticle.php?id=306

Vipond, Mary. 1989. *The mass media in Canada*. Toronto: James Lorimer.

Warner, Michael. 1994. "The mass public and the mass subject." In *Habermas and the public sphere*, edited by Craig Calhoun, 377–401. Cambridge, MA: MIT Press.

Williams, Raymond. 1989. *On television: Selected writings*. New York: Routledge.

Yale, Janet. 2002. "You can't compete with free." Speech delivered at Broadcast Executives Society luncheon, September 19. Available: http//www.digital-homeusa.com/forum/showthread.php?=13646.

Zelkovich, Chris. 2004a. "CBC's movie programming not far off hockey audience." *Toronto Star*, October 19, E10.

Zelkovich, Chris. 2004b. "Only CBC wants TV sports." *Toronto Star*, June 18, E9.

INDEX

OP/POSITION: ISSUES AND IDEAS SERIES

ISSN 1910-1112

As Canadians, we embrace the freedom to talk openly about issues of public concern, one of the fundamental rights of a democratic
society. This series poses hard questions about these often-difficult issues and the directions in which Canadian society should be heading.
It aims to inform Canadians and to stimulate discussion about a variety of hotly debated topics such as globalization, free trade, terrorism
and defence policy, privacy and the Internet, gay rights, reproductive
technologies, same-sex marriage, Native land claims, genetic modifi-
cation, media ownership, poverty and welfare, and disability policy.
These are issues that cut to our core values, evoking a wide range of
opinions and emotions. This series will confront topics such as these
head-on, challenging conventional wisdom and presenting alternative
views.

Canadian Television Today • Bart Beaty and Rebecca Sullivan • No. 1